How
Baseball
Explains
America

Hal Bodley

TRIUMPH
BOOKS

Praise for Hal Bodley and
How Baseball Explains America

Hal Bodley has spent more than half a century chronicling a game he truly loves and understands. Baseball's history is rich, and remarkably, Hal has experienced a good bit of it first-hand.

—Bob Costas, NBC Sports and MLB Network

Hal Bodley had the job we all wanted—and made the most of it. Covering major league baseball with style, wit, and a deep understanding of the game. Now he shares all those years and all those highlights with his many fans. It's almost like being at the ballpark. Just make sure Hal buys the hot dogs.

—Tom Brokaw, former NBC news anchor
and author of *The Greatest Generation*

Hal Bodley loves baseball and Hal Bodley knows baseball—he's been reporting it for over 55 years! He's always had a knack for bringing the game's greatest moments to life. *How Baseball Explains America* is a game-winning home run—in the bottom of the ninth!

—Tim McCarver, Hall of Fame broadcaster

Hal Bodley is one of the most knowledgeable and respected baseball writers I know. His passion for the game and his expertise in reporting it always shows through his articles and columns. *How Baseball Explains America* is invaluable and fascinating.

—Charlie Manuel, former MLB manager

I can think of no better authority than Hal Bodley, the pre-eminent baseball writer in America—going back to the '50s and still going strong!—to explain first-hand what baseball has meant to the nation. This will go down as one of the most important books ever written on baseball.

— Bill Madden, *New York Daily News*

Praise for Hal Bodley and
How Baseball Explains America

For as long as I've been covering baseball, Hal Bodley has been a friend, a mentor, and one of the pillars of modern baseball writing.

—Jayson Stark, ESPN senior writer

In this era of technology, baseball gets caught up in numbers instead of the beauty of the game. In *How Baseball Explains America* Hal Bodley uses his half-century of experience to paint a portrait of our great game for all to enjoy.

**—Joe Torre, former All-Star player
and Hall of Fame manager**

Hal Bodley is the dean of American baseball writers and his over 55 years of experience and insight show in *How Baseball Explains America*. Few baseball reporters have gained the respect Hal has and his work ethic and love for the game is the reason why.

—Don Zimmer, former MLB player and manager

Hal Bodley has done it all in baseball: interviewing, writing, and reporting. His book, *How Baseball Explains America,* interweaves that baseball knowledge with his love and passion for the game, with an understanding of how important the game of baseball is to the American way of life.

**—Dallas Green, former MLB executive and manager;
author of *The Mouth That Roared***

The mutual respect that has existed for years between Hal Bodley and baseball's players and coaches, commissioners, and front-office executives makes everything he writes about our game insightful and relevant.

—Joe Maddon, Tampa Bay Rays manager

Library of Congress Cataloging-in-Publication Data

Bodley, Hal.
  How baseball explains America / Hal Bodley.
      pages cm.
  ISBN 978-1-60078-938-0
  1. Baseball—United States. 2. Baseball—Social aspects—United States. I. Title.
  GV863.A1B62 2014
  796.3570973—dc23
                                                2013051039

This book is available in quantity at special discounts for your group or organization. For further information, contact:

Triumph Books LLC
814 North Franklin Street
Chicago, Illinois 60610
(312) 337-0747
www.triumphbooks.com

Printed in U.S.A.
ISBN: 978-1-60078-938-0
Design by Patricia Frey
Photos courtesy of Getty Images unless otherwise indicated

For Patricia
and
Charles V. Williams, mentor extraordinaire

Contents

Foreword

Among the many craftsmen of baseball journalism, few have been able to match the sweep of Hal Bodley's career. Think about this: Baseball has had two eras. The Dead Ball Era ended around 1920. Hal's career has encompassed most of the subsequent era, which means he has been on the job for most of what we consider modern baseball.

More than half a century ago, when Hal Bodley began making his considerable contributions to baseball, there were 16 major league teams. Until 1955, the western-most teams had been on the western bank of the Mississippi River. But in 1958, when young Hal Bodley arrived on the scene, the National Pastime— the capital letters are still appropriate—became truly national by arriving on the West Coast.

In 1958, the National League pennant was won by the Milwaukee Braves who, having come west from Boston six years earlier, would soon be heading south to Atlanta. Baseball was, like the perennially restless nation, on the move, and Hal was going to chronicle the journey.

It has been a wonderful ride for him, and for those of us who have ridden along with him as his readers. Make no mistake about this: Baseball fans are readers. Today's fans can watch Major

League Baseball on all those things we refer to as our "devices"—personal computers, cell phones, tablets. This is wonderful; it is not, however, sufficient.

Because baseball is a game of distinct episodes—pitch by pitch, out by out—it is a game not just to be seen but also to be savored in the writings about it. Baseball leaves its mark on our mental retinas; it is seen on the replay of our memories.

It has been well said that God gave us memory so we could have roses in winter. I think God gave us Hal Bodley so we could have baseball in winter. And so in 2014 we could have baseball from the 1960s, 1970s, 1980s, 1990s, and 2000s.

In the 1958 All-Star Game, the American Leaguers managed by Casey Stengel beat the National Leaguers managed by Fred Haney 4–3—and the game lasted just two hours and 13 minutes. The rosters included a slew of future Hall of Famers—Willie Mays, Stan Musial, Hank Aaron, Ernie Banks, Bill Mazeroski, Warren Spahn, Eddie Mathews, and Richie Ashburn from the National League, and from the American League Nellie Fox, Mickey Mantle, Luis Aparicio, Yogi Berra, Ted Williams, Al Kaline, Whitey Ford, and Early Wynn. But the real fun in revisiting those rosters, back when the world and Hal (and I) were young, is to remember the lesser names. Eddie Mathews did not start at third base for the National League. Frank Thomas did. Ted Williams was not the American League's starting left fielder. Bob Cerv was. Gus Triandos was the American League's starting catcher while Yogi Berra watched.

When we re-encounter the names of players who burned brightly but briefly, we see the rich weave of baseball's ever-thickening tapestry. Baseball's best writers, of whom Hal Bodley is one, do not just write the game's narrative. The best of them become part of the narrative. Imagine baseball without the writers like Hal Bodley who bring us each season as it unfolds, and who enable us to revisit past seasons, keeping them green in memory.

You are holding in your hand a nourishing buffet of baseball treats. So, turn this page and get started. But do not start late in an evening because you will find it wonderfully difficult to stop.

—George F. Will

1

The Greatest Decade

Tom Brokaw's superb award-winning 1998 book *The Greatest Generation* talks about the stories of a generation, about what "this generation of Americans meant to history."

He said, "It is, I believe, the greatest generation any society has ever produced."

I grew up in that generation and some 65 years later as I look back, Tom's assessment couldn't be more accurate. That generation's greatest time of struggle and triumph was the 1940s, and there is no decade that explains modern baseball in America better than the 1940s. It is the birthplace of the game—and much of the society—we see today.

In 2012 the venerable *Baseball Digest*—the oldest, continuously published baseball magazine in the United States—celebrated its 70th anniversary. It honored that occasion by commissioning a group of national baseball writers to chronicle the events of seven decades, each defined by historic events in the sport.

In the 1950s, after the color barrier was broken in 1947, integration opened the door for great players. The 1960s brought historic moments, including Bill Mazeroski's World Series–winning homer and Roger Maris passing Babe Ruth's fabled home run record of 60. The designated hitter "experiment" came in the

1970s. Pete Rose shattered Ty Cobb's career hits record in the 1980s. Baseball returned from the devastating 1994–95 strike and Cal Ripken Jr. surpassed Lou Gehrig's consecutive-games record in the 1990s. And sadly, steroids, which helped inflate long-standing records, dominated the 2000s.

No period, however, equaled the 1940s.

During an unsettled decade when America was at war, baseball was a desperately needed antidote.

"What's so remarkable is that the players who were part of the Greatest Generation fought in World War II and before and after gave us baseball's greatest decade," Brokaw told me.

In our country's darkest moments, baseball has been an escape, preserving and helping us get through difficult times.

The events of this decade, with so many players going off to war, are firmly etched in the fabric of the greatest game ever invented. You cannot tell about baseball without the 1940s.

A sampling:

- The closest anyone has come to Joe DiMaggio's enduring 56-game hitting streak was Pete Rose in 1978, who was stopped after 44 games.
- Ted Williams batted .406 in 1941, the last player to hit .400 or better during a season.
- The Yankees won five American League pennants and four World Series during the decade.
- The St. Louis Cardinals won four National League pennants and three World Series. They were the last NL team to play in three consecutive (1942–44) World Series.
- Judge Kenesaw Mountain Landis, baseball's first commissioner, died on November 25, 1944.
- On April 15, 1947, Jackie Robinson broke baseball's color barrier, starting for the Brooklyn Dodgers.
- Babe Ruth died on August 16, 1948.

Players the likes of Williams, DiMaggio, Bob Feller, Jerry Coleman, et al, all went off to World War II. Regardless, baseball was, yes, our national pastime—America's game—in that decade.

"The war was interspersed with all of this," Jerry Coleman told me before his death in January 2014. Coleman's entrance into professional baseball was delayed because of World War II. When he finally made it to the Yankees he became Rookie of the Year in 1949.

"Yes, it was a decade that had enormous impact on the game," said Coleman, who was a Marine Corps aviator and after serving in the Korean War became the only major league player to have seen combat in two wars.

Nicknamed "The Colonel," Jerry flew in 120 combat missions and received many honors, including two Distinguished Flying Crosses.

"So much happened in that decade," he said. "When you went to Spring Training with the Yankees, they gave you a number. If you were over 38 you were in the minor leagues. I didn't think I was going to make the club in 1949 because they gave me 42.

"The late Howard Cosell introduced me once: 'Gerald Francis Coleman, number 42—the wrong 42!' I almost punched him."

Jackie Robinson, of course, also wore No. 42, which in 1997 was retired throughout the major leagues.

I'm often reminded of moments in our home in 1941 when the old AM radio crackled each morning with news that The Streak was still alive.

DiMaggio got another hit.

My mom and dad would switch the wooden Philco on and twist the dial up and down, searching for an audible New York station that would tell us, even with all the static, if the Yankee Clipper had extended his amazing streak.

It was that way for much of June and half of July in 1941. Between May 15 and July 16, DiMaggio hit in 56 consecutive games.

More than 70 years have passed since an uneasy America was obsessed with this baseball feat that is yet to be surpassed.

To suggest DiMaggio's hitting streak defined the decade of the 1940s is obviously an exaggeration. But is there a better place to start? It was undoubtedly the signature achievement of DiMaggio's Hall of Fame career.

He was as much an American icon as a ballplayer.

"DiMaggio was the greatest all-around player I ever saw," Ted Williams once told me.

Regardless, baseball was, yes, our national pastime—America's game—in that decade.

"Baseball's greatest decade?" John Thorn, Major League Baseball's official historian, repeated the question. "Some will say the '20s, with the Yankees of Murderers' Row. Others will pipe up for the '60s, with Mantle and Maris, Mays and McCovey, Koufax and Drysdale," he said. "But give me the 1940s, baseball's most tumultuous decade, in which so many things ended and so much began."

Thorn believes nothing during the decade was more important than Jackie Robinson opening a new era in the game while closing a long span of institutionalized bigotry.

"That's the great, enduring legacy of the 1940s," he said. "But in this time we also saw the last .400 hitter, the unchallenged 56-game hit streak, the peak of minor league baseball, the dawn of televised ballgames, and more.

"I agree that at no time in the game's history was baseball so unquestionably seen as America's Game. By that I mean in the years of struggle during World War II, and then the glorious burst of relief and optimism in the last years of the decade. American had prevailed, and with it baseball and its promise of a better tomorrow."

Dr. Bobby Brown, now 89 (turning 90 on October 25, 2014), was a third baseman for the Yankees for eight seasons beginning in 1946. He served with the U.S. Navy from July 1, 1943, through January 17, 1946.

Brown, a cardiologist for 25 years after baseball, later became president of the American League (1984–1994). He and Yogi Berra are the only living members of the Yankees who won the 1947 World Series.

"World War II ended in August of 1945 and our whole country was euphoric," Brown told me. "People were looking for some relief from all that tension. The ballplayers began to filter back who were in the service and this was so important for our country."

Brown believes about 95 percent of all major leaguers served.

"This was a unique time because everyone was ready for something like that." No decade was more important, had more impact on baseball, he added.

"Professional baseball at that time had no real competition from either football or basketball," he said. "Baseball was at the forefront. The 1940s were just great; there are so many historic memories from that decade. It was about America."

Hall of Famer Ralph Kiner believes "the late 1940s was definitely the heyday for Major League Baseball. Players were coming back from the war and it took time for them to return to their prime, but they did. They had so much to prove and it was exciting."

In a sense baseball helped America exorcise the trauma of the war.

Just a little over a month after Pearl Harbor, on January 15, 1942, President Franklin Delano Roosevelt wrote his "Green Light" letter to Commissioner Landis.

"I honestly feel it would be best for the country to keep baseball going," Roosevelt wrote.

FDR eliminated any doubt how important, what an outlet, baseball was. It became a soothing factor.

Hall of Famer Bob Feller won 25 games in 1941 and didn't pitch again for Cleveland until 1945. The day after the Sunday, December 7, 1941, bombing of Pearl Harbor he refused to use his 3-C draft deferment and enlisted in the Navy.

He thus became the first MLB player to enlist in World War II, and missed nearly four seasons of baseball at the height of his career. He returned for nine games in 1945 and won 26 the following summer with an uncanny 2.18 earned run average.

"To this day, I'm proud of that decision," he told me in 2008. "It was important to serve my country.

"But baseball interest never waned during the war," said Feller, who died on December 15, 2010, at age 92. "A lot of the players who stayed home were 4-F [physically ineligible for the draft]. Hal Newhouser had a leaky heart; Lou Boudreau had bad ankles.

"When I was at sea, which I was for 34 months as the gun captain on the battleship *Alabama*—we took supplies to Russia—I was in the radio shack all the time—trying to follow the games and get the scores. It was so important. And whenever I could, I played catch aboard the ship."

He was quick to add during this conversation that "baseball was strengthened by how important the game also was to those not fighting overseas. It was necessary for the people working in the factories for the games to continue. A very smart move."

The late Leonard Koppett, in his exhausting history of Major League Baseball, wrote that "of all American institutions, the two fundamental items of mass entertainment, Hollywood movies and Major League Baseball, probably changed the least during World War II."

Before Pearl Harbor, the decade was off to a rousing start.

In 1941, of course, DiMaggio hit safely in an incredible 56 consecutive games. In Cleveland's spacious Municipal Stadium he collected No. 56 on July 16, in a game in which he had a double and two singles.

The next day, with some 67,000 fans in attendance, the streak ended. He grounded out on a close play, walked, grounded out, and in the eighth inning hit a bouncer that shortstop Lou Boudreau turned into a double play. The streak was over.

After it ended, Joe D. hit in each of the next 16 games, thus hitting safely in 72 of 73.

The Yankees, who would go on to win the World Series over Brooklyn in five games, won three out of every four games played during DiMaggio's streak. He had 91 hits in the 56 games, batted .408, hit 15 homers, and drove in 55 runs.

And there was Williams' .406 batting average.

On the final day of the season Williams' average was .3995. Teammates and friends tried to talk him into sitting out the game because the final average would have been rounded out to .400.

Williams wouldn't have any of that. He played both games of a doubleheader against the Philadelphia A's, went 6-for-8 and finished with the .406 average.

In the ballot for the MVP that year it was DiMaggio who won the award.

When it was announced, Ted said, "Yeah, awright, but it took the Big Guy to beat me."

So this is how it was on the eve of Pearl Harbor.

During a long sit-down interview with Williams in the early 1990s, he talked to me about the years he lost (1943–45) during World War II. (He also lost most of two seasons, 1952–53, when he was called back by the Marine Corps to be a fighter pilot.)

After Pearl Harbor was attacked, he tried to get a draft deferment, but in May 1942 enlisted in the air arm of the Marine Corps, hoping not to be called up right away. He completed the '42 season, winning the AL batting title with a .356 average, the home run title (36), and the RBI crown (137) to take the Triple Crown.

After three years, he came back in 1946 and hit .342, with 38 homers and 123 RBI. He led the Boston Red Sox to their first AL pennant in 28 years.

Feller, Hank Greenberg, et al, were already in the service in 1942, but DiMaggio, because he was a married father with a child, received a deferment and played in '42. His brother, Dom, had already signed up.

Joe was reluctant to enter the service. There was pressure from his wife, Dorothy, for him to sign up. Finally, he entered the Army Air Corps in 1943. He basically spent three years playing baseball on the base team, first in California near Los Angeles, then in Hawaii. He spent time in and out of hospitals where he was treated for ulcers. Some speculate his ulcers may have been a result of going through a divorce from Dorothy.

"The war years never seemed to move at all," he once said. "I thought they would never end."

Even though DiMaggio was discharged from the Army Air Corps early, he sat out the 1945 season, recovering from the ulcers and stomach problems. He returned in 1946, but struggled, even though he hit .290, with 95 RBI and 25 homers.

Red Sox Hall of Famer Bobby Doerr a nine-time All-Star, was typical.

He spent the 1945 season in the military, but when he returned in 1946 he led the Red Sox to the AL pennant with 18 homers and 116 runs batted in. He hit .409 and drove in three more runs in Boston's World Series loss to the Cardinals.

Joe Garagiola spent parts of three seasons (1944–46) in military service.

He'd spent three seasons in the minors, but when he returned to the St. Louis Cardinals on May 20, 1946, he became the starting catcher on a team that would go on to win the National League pennant and beat the Boston Red Sox in the World Series.

Garagiola, who later became a Hall of Fame broadcaster, hit .316 in the seven-game World Series.

"There was a lot of outstanding baseball played after the war," Garagiola told me in an interview for the *Baseball Digest* story.

"The big thing was there were only eight teams in each league. A lot of the guys had things to prove to themselves. There weren't any guaranteed contracts then."

In 1946, the Cardinals and Dodgers tied for the NL pennant, causing a best-of-three playoff for the first time in the history of baseball. Both the Cardinals and Dodgers won 96 games.

The nucleus of the Cardinals consisted of outfielder Stan Musial—he was switched to first base on June 7—second baseman Red Schoendienst, outfielder Enos "Country" Slaughter, pitcher Howie Pollet and, of course, Garagiola.

"We had a big rivalry with the Dodgers," Garagiola said. "The last day of the season we were doing a lot of scoreboard watching, but we both ended in a first-place tie."

"I remember Dodgers manager Leo Durocher [who had the choice] decided to open the playoff series in St. Louis so they could clinch it in Brooklyn," Garagiola said with a chuckle. "It didn't work out that way. We won the game in St. Louis 4–2, and in Brooklyn 8–4.

"We were also underdogs in the World Series, but won it all over Boston in seven games."

Garagiola played in just 77 games in 1947 and was sent to the minors after 24 games in 1948. He made it back to the Cardinals in 1949, batting .261, and then hit .318 in 34 games in 1950, but a severe shoulder separation ended his season.

"The 1940s was a good decade to play in, especially now—when you can talk about it," he said. "There were some great players. Broadcasting was different. We had none of that interviewing players or managers during the game, no mascots.

"In the 1940s guys didn't fool around on the mound as they do now. There were no 100-pitch limits. The bullpen was a place where guys went to pitch themselves back into the rotation. I don't remember any closers or holders or anything like that. When pitchers went out they wanted to finish the game. They never looked at the bullpen. A hundred pitches didn't mean anything then. In those days, because there were just eight teams, every ballclub had three good pitchers."

Joe was on a roll now, looking back with fascination in his voice.

"I don't want to sound like an old player, but it was very intense in those days," he said. "Unlike today, they didn't bring this guy up for two games, then send him back or anything like that. They didn't rent players; they went with what they had.

"The other thing I miss a lot watching the games," he bubbled. "Guys would talk it up a little bit, not screaming at each other. But there was more chatter in the infield. Now, it's like walking across a cemetery at midnight. You don't hear anything.

"And this: Did you ever think you'd see a hitter strike out in a game, then run right into the clubhouse and look at video to see what he did wrong?"

———

By 1947 television was beginning its huge media impact on baseball. Of the 16 teams, only the Pittsburgh Pirates hadn't negotiated a local TV deal to carry home games. Road games weren't televised then because the cost of cables was too high.

But as our national pastime recovered from World War II and prepared for a new decade, nothing had the immediate and forever impact of Jackie Robinson becoming the first black player in the major leagues on April 15, 1947.

Famed black journalist Doc Young of the Cleveland *Call and Post* wrote: "Rickey planned Robinson's entrance as carefully as a man would build a house with match sticks."

It was so important that on the 50th anniversary of Robinson breaking the barrier, Commissioner Bud Selig ordered his No. 42 be retired by every major league team and displayed in each ballpark.

From that moment on, Jackie Robinson Day has been observed throughout the majors each year.

In 1945, as the war was ending, Brooklyn Dodgers president Branch Rickey quietly began searching for the perfect African American to play in the major leagues. He zeroed in on Robinson. Secretly, he signed Jackie to a 1946 minor league contract. Robinson spent the '46 season with Montreal, the Dodgers Triple A farm club, where he batted .349 with 40 stolen bases.

He went to Spring Training the following year with the Dodgers and the rest is history.

Maverick owner Bill Veeck, who bought the Cleveland Indians in 1947, had long had inner thoughts of integrating the major leagues. His first thought was the ageless Satchel Paige.

But with Robinson already playing for the Dodgers in the National League, Veeck signed Larry Doby, who became the first black player in the American League on July 5, 1947, when he started for the Indians.

Both Robinson and Doby are in the Hall of Fame.

The legacy of the 1940s?

Commissioner Bud Selig likes to say we are now in the Golden Era of Baseball. The commissioner may be correct, but the foundation for it was laid in the 1940s.

The 1940s brought us the birth of televised games and the breaking of the color barrier, all while DiMaggio and Williams were etching numbers in the baseball record book that still stand today. And for the opportunity to do those great deeds on the diamond, those same men went around the world to fight the Axis and make the world and our country safe for democracy.

No one has yet figured out exactly when baseball was invented, but the modern game we know and love today was forged in the crucible of the 1940s.

2

Drugs on the Street, Drugs on the Diamond

In 1998, Major League Baseball was groping for a big moment; it desperately needed an enduring victory.

Effects of the devastating 1994–95 players' strike were still being felt even though Cal Ripken Jr.'s shattering of Lou Gehrig's consecutive games record in 1995 had given the sport a huge lift.

But what baseball really needed as it approached a new century was a tantalizing event, a happening that would reach deep into America and captivate die-hard fans and non-fans alike.

Along came Mark McGwire and Sammy Sosa, their home runs exploding throughout the summer and energizing the sport.

Their home run chase of Roger Maris' season record of 61, set in 1961, became a Madison Avenue dream. It was riveting theater at its best.

The 1998 season was elevated to unbelievable heights.

Home runs off the bats of Sosa, the fun-loving, charismatic Chicago Cubs outfielder, and McGwire, the St. Louis Cardinals hulking, aristocratic first baseman, became the sports story of the year.

It became the Sosa-McGwire "love fest."

Sosa's effervescent personality during media sessions with McGwire (when the Cubs played the Cardinals) seemed to energize Mark, who earlier in the season was uncomfortable and cold talking to reporters about his feats.

Sosa-McGwire became a phenomenon in 1998.

But on an otherwise normal game day in August of that summer, Steve Wilstein, an Associated Press reporter, looked in Mark McGwire's locker and his eyes stopped at a bottle of androstenedione.

Androstenedione? Let's call it Andro.

It's a pill that was sold over the counter in 1998 that produces male hormone for the intended purpose of building muscle mass. The dietary supplement was designed to mimic a steroid.

We didn't know it—and even criticized Wilstein's snooping, but from that moment on baseball's "Steroids Era" was born.

With Roger Maris' widow, Patricia, and her sons in the stands, McGwire surpassed Roger's record at Busch Stadium against the Cubs' Steve Trachsel on September 8.

A Hollywood screenwriter couldn't have done better—putting McGwire and Sosa on the Busch Stadium field together the same night the record was broken.

It was a joyous occasion.

Bud Selig, elected permanent commissioner earlier that summer, sat next to Stan Musial and later recalled how excited he was when McGwire's ball sailed over the left-field wall for his 62nd homer. The slugger went on to hit 70 in 1998, 65 the next season, and ended a 16-year career with 583.

Sosa hit 66 home runs in the year he battled McGwire, 63 in 1999, and 609 during an 18-year career.

But a dark cloud was forming.

The decade of the 1990s became one of the most remarkable offensive eras in baseball's history.

Was it legitimate?

Congress, with such influential members as Sen. Jim Bunning, the Hall of Fame pitcher, voicing concerns and summoning baseball officials to hearings was sending a strong message.

Selig was concerned about Andro, but admittedly ignorant on the subject. After all, anyone could walk into a GNC store and purchase a bottle. The supplement was legal, a strong claim the players union made.

To his credit and throughout his term, Selig has never been one to turn his back on a problem. Often slow to reach a decision, his determination to research all facts on any issue facing baseball has frequently irritated those close to him.

"He's never satisfied until he has every minute detail before commenting or reaching a decision. His greatest ability is to build consensus, but to achieve that he demands all the facts," a former MLB executive told me. "He's very demanding and that can be extremely frustrating. Bud just won't let up sometimes."

During the winter of 2000 he summoned a group of major league trainers and medical personnel to his Milwaukee office.

In essence, Selig wanted to be educated on Steroids 101.

He remembers how the meeting dragged on.

Finally, the commissioner raised his hand.

"What is the most serious problem, the main concern in our sport?" he asked.

There was little hesitation from around the table.

The extensive, growing use of anabolic steroids, Selig was told.

Loud and clear, the medical folks got the commissioner's attention.

When I started covering baseball in 1958, amphetamines—"greenies" as they were called—were prevalent in virtually every baseball clubhouse.

As Howard Bryant wrote in his excellent 2005 book *Juicing the Game*, "Amphetamines were baseball's open secret…. Amphetamine use had been tacitly condoned in major league clubhouses for 40 years."

Dr. Theodosios (Ted) Soldatos, an internist who's practiced in the Gainesville, Florida, area for nearly two decades, believes drug problems in baseball and other sports have mirrored those in our society at large.

"I think it's absurd to think there's a difference, that baseball is separate from our overall society," said Soldatos, who grew up in

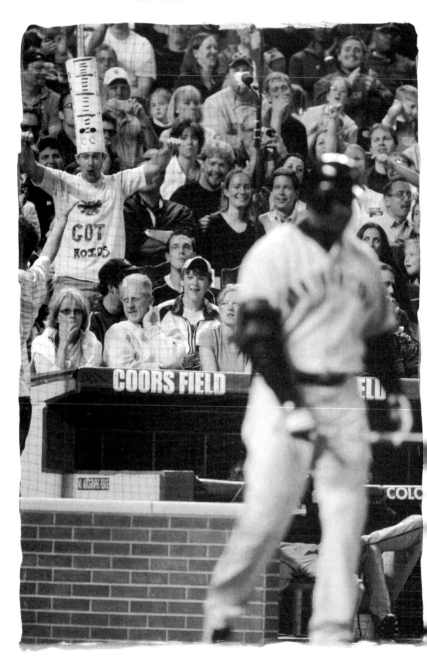

Toronto as a passionate hockey fan, but followed baseball closely while going to undergraduate school at Boston University. "I see evidence of this every day with my patients."

Soldatos is probably more exposed to this because of the location of his practice. Gainesville, of course, is the home of the University of Florida.

"I know there's a major concern about steroids and amphetamines, but I firmly believe the so-called 'designer drugs' and prescription drugs are also a huge problem.

"It's so difficult because I have patients who come into the office either with pain or anxiety or depression," he told me during an extensive interview. "In this era, you have to be careful of what to prescribe. I repeatedly have to ask the question, 'What are the chances of them, especially young athletes, getting addicted?'"

In November 2013, Florida representative Trey Radel announced he was taking a leave of absence after he pled guilty in Washington, D.C., Superior Court, charged with cocaine possession. He said he needs treatment for "addiction issues."

And on January 27, 2014, he ended a once promising career when he resigned from Congress.

Remember Dock Ellis?

On June 12, 1970—under the influence of LSD, he later revealed—he pitched a no-hitter for the Pirates against the San Diego Padres.

The Pirates flew to San Diego on June 11 for their four-game series against the Padres. Ellis said he visited a friend in Los Angeles that night and used LSD "two or three times."

Thinking it was still Thursday, he took a hit of LSD on Friday at noon, and his girlfriend reminded him at 2:00 PM that he was scheduled to pitch that night at San Diego Stadium. Ellis flew from Los Angeles to San Diego at 3:00 PM and arrived at the ballpark at 4:30 PM, with the game starting at 6:05 PM.

He threw the no-hitter despite, he said, not being able to feel the ball or see the batter or catcher clearly.

Ellis said catcher Jerry May wore reflective tape on his fingers which helped him see May's signals. Ellis walked eight batters and struck out six, and was aided by excellent fielding plays by second baseman Bill Mazeroski and center fielder Matty Alou.

"I can only remember bits and pieces of the game," said Ellis, who died in 2008 from liver disease. "I was psyched. I had a feeling of euphoria. I was zeroed in on the catcher's glove, but I didn't hit the glove too much. I remember hitting a couple of batters, and the bases were loaded two or three times.

"The ball was small at times, it was large sometimes and sometimes I saw the catcher and sometimes I didn't. Sometimes I tried to stare the hitter down and throw while I was looking at him. I chewed my gum until it turned to powder."

And then there was this: "I started having a crazy idea in the fourth inning that Richard Nixon was the home-plate umpire, and once I thought I was pitching a baseball to Jimi Hendrix, who to me was holding a guitar and swinging it over the plate. They say I had about three to four fielding chances. I remember diving out of the way of a ball I thought was a line drive. I jumped, but the ball wasn't hit hard and never reached me."

Ellis said he never used LSD during the season again, but continued to heavily use amphetamines. He said he began drinking alcohol and using drugs when he was 14. After his retirement in 1979, he revealed he never pitched without the use of drugs.

He underwent treatment and remained sober and devoted the remainder of his life to counseling drug addicts at treatment centers and prisons.

Dr. Soldatos reminded me of the 2003 death of Baltimore Orioles pitcher Steve Bechler in Spring Training.

"The young man's death prompted a study of the effects of the supplement ephedra," said Soldatos. "The Food and Drug Administration took action regarding ephedra products."

Bechler died of heatstroke, although an autopsy concluded his death was caused by abnormal liver function and mild hypertension, his weight problem (he weighed 320 pounds and was exercising hard), the fact that he was not used to South Florida's warm weather, and the toxicity of ephedra.

Bechler was using the supplement ephedra against the advice of his trainer, according to Wikipedia.

And of course, not to be forgotten, there's Ken Caminiti, an All-Star who was the 1996 National League MVP. Caminiti, only 41, died of a cocaine and heroin overdose on October 10, 2004.

He'd struggled with substance abuse throughout his career. In a *Sports Illustrated* cover story in 2002, a year after his retirement, he admitted that he had used steroids during his MVP season and several years after that. He also had a long struggle with cocaine.

Just five days before his death, he told a Houston court that he had violated his probation. He had tested positive for cocaine on September 2004, his fourth violation.

He was in the apartment of a friend in New York on October 10, and after having what is called a "speedball" of cocaine and heroin, collapsed and died at the hospital. The autopsy results stated that "acute intoxication due to the combined effects of cocaine and opiates caused his death."

Cocaine?

In the 1980s, it was a cocaine epidemic that became the hot-button topic, climaxing with the highly publicized Pittsburgh Drug Trials.

Peter Ueberroth, highly successful chairman of the 1984 Los Angeles Summer Olympics, succeeded Bowie Kuhn as baseball commissioner on October 1, 1984.

Soon after taking office, Ueberroth was thrown into the middle of the game's escalating cocaine problem.

As a reporter, I first began to hear of players using illegal drugs during the latter years of Kuhn's regime. Los Angeles Dodgers relief pitcher Steve Howe had a problem and was more than once suspended.

To his credit, Kuhn, who was ultimately not re-elected by major league owners, tried to take a strong stance against the game's drug-related problems. Actually, he implemented the first drug-related policy, but it was mostly ineffective and challenged by Major League Players Association guru Marvin Miller and his successor, Don Fehr.

Regardless, I remember several sessions in Kuhn's office and how he stressed the importance of maintaining the integrity and image of baseball.

SteroidsinBaseball.net is an excellent source for the details of early drug use while Kuhn was in office:

- In 1983, players Willie Mays Aikens, Jerry Martin, Vida Blue, and Willie Wilson pled guilty to the misdemeanor charges of attempted cocaine possession. Each served three months in jail. Upon their release, Kuhn suspended them from baseball for one year without pay. (Although some of the sentences were later modified in arbitration, Kuhn's actions clearly defined his stance as one who would neither condone nor forgive player involvement in illegal activities.)
- Pitcher Steve Howe had completed his first drug treatment in 1983, only to fail two drug tests. Kuhn suspended him from baseball after each failure.
- In 1984, Braves pitcher Pascual Perez was arrested in the Dominican Republic for cocaine possession. Upon his return to the U.S., Kuhn suspended him for one month. (Perez filed a grievance with the player's union, and his punishment was subsequently overturned.)

Aikens played baseball for three different teams from 1977 to 1985. Most of those years were with the Royals. Cocaine became a curse for the talented player. After his playing days were over, he was caught selling crack cocaine to an undercover policeman and sentenced to over 20 years in prison.

During a recent interview with writer Kevin J. Wells, Aikens, drug free for 20 years and now a Royals minor league hitting coach said, "The first time I tried cocaine was 1979 as a member of the California Angels and I only did it once. After I got traded to the Royals, you know, there were some guys on the team that used to party, liked to get high. So I just became part of that group. My years of using coke in the major leagues was like 1980 to 1983 when I was with Kansas City…. I never used drugs during the game. It was always after the game…. You know, cocaine is a stimulant, so when you do it after the game, it lingers in your system up until the next game, but I never used it before a game in the clubhouse."

The Pittsburgh Drug Trials of 1985 were the catalyst for a baseball-related cocaine scandal which resulted in the harshest penalties at the time in Major League Baseball since the 1919 Chicago Black Sox scandal.

Dale Berra, Lee Lacy, Lee Mazzilli, John Milner, Dave Parker, and Rod Scurry of the Pittsburgh Pirates and others, including Aikens, Vida Blue, Enos Cabell, Keith Hernandez, Jeffrey Leonard, Tim Raines, and Lonnie Smith, were subpoenaed to appear before a Pittsburgh grand jury.

Their testimony led to the highly publicized drug trials, which dominated baseball in September 1985.

The players were granted immunity in exchange for their testimony.

Ex-Pirate John Milner talked about getting amphetamines from Hall of Famers Willie Mays and Willie Stargell. Milner added that he bought two grams of cocaine for $200 in the bathroom stalls at Three Rivers Stadium during a Pirates-Astros game in 1980.

Hernandez added that about 40 percent of all major leaguers were using cocaine at the time. Hernandez however, quickly backtracked by saying that he might have been "grossly wrong." Raines told how he'd keep a gram of coke in his uniform pocket (as well as revealing that he snorted during games), and that he only slid into bases headfirst so as not to break the vial.

Testimony also revealed that Scurry once went looking for cocaine during the late innings of a Pirates game. Drug dealers frequented the Pirates' clubhouse. Even the Pirate Parrot mascot, Kevin Koch, was implicated for buying cocaine and introducing a few of the ballplayers to a local drug dealer.

Curtis Strong and six Pittsburgh men were convicted and found guilty of 11 counts of distributing cocaine. Strong received a 12-year prison sentence, but was released after serving just four years.

I attended a major press conference at the Waldorf Astoria in New York on February 28, 1986, when Ueberroth handed down suspensions to 11 players—seven for a full season. The players who were suspended for a full year were allowed to play under the condition that they donated 10 percent of their base salaries to drug-related community service, submitted to random drug testing, and contributed 100 hours of drug-related community service.

Those seven were Joaquin Andujar, Dale Berra, Enos Cabell, Keith Hernandez, Jeffrey Leonard, Dave Parker, and Lonnie Smith.

The four players—Al Holland, Lee Lacy, Lary Sorensen, and Claudell Washington—who were suspended for just 60 days were allowed to play if they donated five percent of their base salaries and contributed 50 hours of drug-related community service.

Ueberroth also asked every player to submit to voluntary urine tests. Ultimately, the players union thwarted that plea.

For the better part of three decades commissioners battled with the powerful players union to get a strong drug program.

Led by executive director Don Fehr and Gene Orza, his No. 1 lieutenant, the union refused to approve any type of drug program that required random testing.

As an aside, Marvin Miller, the Major League Players Association executive director from 1966 to 1982 who transformed the union into one of the strongest the United States, has repeatedly not received enough votes for the Hall of Fame.

Once again, in December 2013, he was snubbed.

Miller, who died on November 27, 2012, repeatedly was opposed to the drug testing of major leaguers. He continued to strongly express those views while in retirement.

I believe in the last election he did not receive support from players on the committee making the decision because the majority of players disagreed with his strong stand. They want the sport cleaned up.

In 1985, as cocaine was dominating the news, Ueberroth enacted a random drug program that included testing. It was to be administered to virtually all baseball personnel, with the exception of the major league players.

"Somebody has to say, 'Enough is enough' against drugs," Ueberroth said. "Baseball is going to accomplish this. It's a tiny little segment of society. We're going to remove drugs and be an example."

Ueberroth, in good faith and maybe a bit naïve, was attempting to put pressure on the players.

Actually, his office didn't consult with the players union before the announcement. Fehr accused Ueberroth of "grandstanding."

A few players backed the plan, but most opposed it.

One was Dale Murphy, the Atlanta Braves' two-time National League MVP.

"It's assuming a guy is guilty without knowing," he said. "I understand there's a problem and we have to try and solve it. It's the principle that's hard for me to accept."

Said Boston pitcher Bob Stanley: "I don't take drugs, and I don't believe I have to piss in a bottle to prove I don't."

I was baseball editor at *USA TODAY* during this period and, sadly, I spent more time chasing stories about drugs and management's sparring with the players union over the subject than reporting the game on the field.

In a May 1985 analysis in *Sports Illustrated*, writers Jim Kaplan and Ivan Maisel wrote that "Ueberroth seemed to be shooting from the hip. He said he would announce more details [about the drug program] on May 20, but did not disclose that employees will submit samples 'twice, maybe three times a year. It will be random testing.'

"Test results, he said, would be kept in strictest confidence and would be used to help rather than punish those with drug problems. Which drugs are the targets? 'Illegal drugs, obviously cocaine, heroin, marijuana, and other types of substances,' said Ueberroth. He was not sure about amphetamines and had no plans to test for anabolic steroids, arguing that 'it is not an illegal substance.'

"But athletes often obtain steroids on the black market and by not testing for them, Ueberroth seemingly contradicts his concern for health of baseball people."

In hindsight his views seem frighteningly naive. In fewer than 15 years the use of steroids would become widespread in baseball, would threaten the credibility of the sport's sacred records, and become one of the biggest problems the game has ever faced.

"The Steroid Era," as that complex time came to be known, was about much more than what happened on the diamond. The steroids/HGH wave of the late-1980s and 1990s not only took over baseball, but was seen everywhere. It's uncanny how baseball's drug problems have been so analogous to those of our society as a whole.

Older men began using performance-enhancing drugs to feel younger. In March 2007, the masculine "Rocky," 60-year-old Sylvester Stallone, was caught at Sydney Airport with several vials of HGH during a random baggage check. Australian customs authorities claim they found a total of 48 vials of the steroids after they raided Stallone's Sydney hotel room, limo, and private jet.

Stallone was visiting Australia to promote his latest movie, *Rocky Balboa*.

Of course, disgraced cyclist Lance Armstrong, after years of denials, admitted that he had used steroids and doped during all of his Tour de France victories. He was banned from all organized sport for life and stripped of his Tour de France titles and Olympic bronze medal.

Yes, while most baseball executives and reporters were allegedly asleep at the wheel, steroids became the game's most pressing issue.

Those of us close to the game, including Commissioner Bud Selig and his lieutenants, didn't know it, but that August afternoon when Steve Wilstein peered into Mark McGwire's locker would ignite one of the most difficult and depressing eras baseball has endured.

From "greenies" to cocaine to the Andro in Mark McGwire's locker to the Congressional finger-wagging of Rafael Palmeiro to Barry Bonds and the BALCO scandal to the full-blown Biogenesis investigation, these have been the potholes, the jarring bumps Major League Baseball has had to cope with the past four decades.

The players' strike, which wiped out the 1994 World Series and extended into 1995, was still a vivid memory when owners and players negotiated a new Collective Bargaining Agreement in 2002.

Drug testing was a key issue in the negotiations.

In early June of that year, I suggested that *USA TODAY* conduct a players' poll about the use of steroids in baseball. We released the poll on July 8, the eve of the All-Star Game in Milwaukee.

I drove from Milwaukee to the Chicago O'Hare Airport Hilton that morning to cover an executive board meeting of the players union. Upon arrival, I was greeted by Fehr, who was incensed by our poll and accompanying story.

He insisted the story had no credibility.

USA TODAY reported that 17 percent of the players polled were against independent random steroid testing, but 79 percent favored random testing.

The poll also disclosed that 44 percent of the players surveyed said they felt pressure to use steroids or other performance-enhancing substances because they wanted what they called a level playing field. It was unfair, they insisted, to keep up with players already using anabolic steroids.

Even though Fehr blasted the report, there was no union-initiated poll of his union members about how the players truly felt or what action they wanted to take about the issue.

Negotiations dragged on that summer, with an August 31 strike deadline set.

I was in New York that day and night, prepared to report that once again the players were walking out. There seemed little hope that a settlement could be reached.

At about 6:00 AM New York time, what I consider a miracle occurred. There would be no strike; games would be played on September 1.

And for the first time in baseball history, there would be testing for steroids, although it was greatly watered down. Had MLB lead negotiator Rob Manfred pressed for a stronger program, which he obviously wanted, there would have been a strike.

It was called the "Survey Test."

Under the agreement, every player in the league would be tested for steroids informally in 2003. They would be tested once and a week later tested again. The test results would be confidential and used only to determine the extent of illegal performance-enhancing drugs in baseball. The union had the right to destroy the test results.

The agreement stated that if more than 5 percent of the survey pool tested positive, Major League Baseball would enact a more stringent program in 2004 with mandatory testing. A first positive then would trigger confidential treatment. Multiple positives would call for suspensions of from 15 to 50 games. A player would be suspended for life if he tested positive five times.

I believe the union ultimately agreed to this program because it was convinced the 5 percent threshold wouldn't be passed.

Surprise!

Of the 1,198 players tested, 104 had positive results; the percentage was between 5 and 7.

So, in 2004 a mandatory drug-testing program was implemented.

After numerous negotiations with the players union, pressure from Congress, and an untiring effort by Selig, the 2004 program has evolved into what the commissioner now labels as the toughest in professional sports.

Even before the Collective Bargaining Agreement was approved on August 31, 2002, BALCO, the Bay Area Laboratory Co-operative, was involved in an investigation by the U.S. Federal Government.

The following investigation of BALCO founder Victor Conte and scores of athletes who purchased supplements, including anabolic steroids, from him became a huge dark cloud that hung over major league baseball for years.

Companies like BALCO are also a reminder of what an uphill battle we fight against drugs.

As MLB develops stronger testing, the methods of evading detection evolve as well. Just as designer drugs are in the streets and clubs and the schools, we see that same ingenuity coming to bear on PEDs, so that they are always morphing, always trying to stay one step ahead of the tests—like the Hydra: cut off one head and another grows.

"That's a terrific analogy," laughed Soldatos, a fan of Greek mythology. "You have big drug dealers getting arrested and put out of business. Then, you have two or three more that pop up. What's happening with designer drugs is you have traffickers and chemists that are altering certain drugs to produce a different drug. The FDA is saying we get rid of one drug by outlawing it, the chemists develop others to skirt the law. So, you get two more new designer drugs for every one banned."

He adds that he's had college football players "come into the office who make me suspicious they're using anabolic steroids. They might complain about a certain ailment that pain medications help. Even at that age, they're trying to get an edge. Before I prescribe anything like that, I check them out thoroughly.

"With today's computerized medical records, I can research these patients to make sure they're not going from one doctor to another, complaining about the same problem in order to get pain medications."

Dr. Soldatos, who "moonlighted" as a prison doctor during his early years in practice, said that "was an awakening for me about the extensive use of drugs in our society."

He added that patients would fake pain and injuries so he'd prescribe painkillers that they were addicted to.

"We have really clamped down on prescribing many of the narcotics. They're more difficult to get on the street now," he said. "I wonder what's going to come out next. Are people going to start going back to cheaper drugs on the market like heroin, etc.? Right now, there's an illegal, synthetic marijuana available even though the government in 2012 banned the ingredients for that."

Soldatos talked at length about steroids and HGH, but said he feels ultimately the illegal use of prescription drugs is probably as big a problem.

And in the summer of 2013, Selig and MLB took their most dramatic action in over two decades of attempts to rid baseball of performance-enhancing substances.

After an extensive, months-long investigation of major leaguers tied to the Anthony Bosch–Biogenesis anti-aging clinic in South

Florida that allegedly provided players with PEDs, 12 players on August 5 accepted 50-game suspensions without pay for violations of the drug program.

Two former MVPs, two of the most prominent players in the game—the Milwaukee Brewers' Ryan Braun, who won his appeal from a 2011 suspension, and the New York Yankees' Alex Rodriguez—were dealt the most severe discipline.

Yes, baseball began drug testing for the 2003 season, added penalties the following year, banned amphetamines in 2006, and started Human Growth Hormone (HGH) blood testing in 2012. Yet, critics insist Major League Baseball didn't move fast enough.

"People say, 'Well, you were slow to react.' We were not slow to react," Selig said. "In fact, I heard that recently, and it aggravates me all over again.

"We continue to attack this issue on every front—from science and research to education and awareness to fact-finding and investigative skills," Selig added. "Major League Baseball is proud of the enormous progress we have made, and we look forward to working with the players to make the penalties for violations of the drug program even more stringent and a stronger deterrent."

In the spring of 2006, former U.S. Senate Majority Leader George Mitchell was commissioned to conduct an independent investigation/examination of baseball to determine how widespread the use of banned substances was.

After 21 months, the Mitchell Report was released. It revealed 89 players were connected to illegal performance-enhancing drugs.

Included in the report were seven-time Cy Young Award–winning pitcher Roger Clemens and seven-time National League MVP Barry Bonds.

Clemens was accused of using steroids and HGH in 1998, 2000, and 2001. He was later acquitted of lying to Congress about his use of PEDs in 2012.

Bonds was convicted in April 2010 by a federal jury in San Francisco of obstructing a U.S. probe of professional athletes. He was sentenced to 30 days of house arrest, probation for two years, and a $4,000 fine.

Jason Giambi, slugging first baseman/designated hitter and former AL MVP, was connected to the BALCO investigation. To his credit, Giambi stood up and apologized. He was not penalized, mostly because MLB did not have a testing program prior to 2003.

In an interview with *USA TODAY*, Giambi said, "I was wrong for using that stuff. What we should have done a long time ago was stand up—players, ownership, everybody—and said, 'We made a mistake.'"

Braun accepted a 65-game suspension without pay that ended his 2013 season.

"I have disappointed the people closest to me—the ones who fought for me because they truly believed me all along," Braun said in a statement. "I kept the truth from everyone. For a long time, I was in denial and convinced myself that I had not done anything wrong."

Rodriguez, the highest-paid player in the history of the game, was hit with a whopping 211-game suspension for what MLB stated "is based on his use and possession of numerous forms of prohibited performance-enhancing substances, including Testosterone and Human Growth Hormone, over the course of multiple years."

A-Rod was also disciplined for "attempting to cover up his violations of the drug program by engaging in a course of conduct intended to obstruct and frustrate the office of the commissioner's investigation." In January 2014, arbitrator Fredric Horowitz reduced the suspension to 162 games, a full season.

The 12 players who accepted 50-game suspensions without appeal: Phillies pitcher Antonio Bastardo, Padres shortstop Everth Cabrera, Yankees catcher Francisco Cervelli, Rangers outfielder Nelson Cruz, Padres pitcher Fautino De Los Santos, Astros pitcher Sergio Escalona, Yankees outfielder Fernando Martinez, Mariners catcher Jesus Montero, free-agent pitcher Jordan Norberto, Tigers shortstop Jhonny Peralta, Mets outfielder Cesar Puello, and Mets infielder-outfielder Jordany Valdespin.

The relationship between owners and players has changed dramatically.

When the suspensions were announced, union executive director Michael Weiner said, "The accepted suspensions announced today are consistent with the punishments set forth in the Joint Drug Agreement, and were arrived at only after hours of intense negotiations between bargaining parties, the players, and their representatives."

Those words, or any agreement over drugs, would not have been uttered 20 years ago.

Weiner, 51, died on November 21, 2013, after being diagnosed with a brain tumor 15 months earlier.

Now, MLB's Joint Drug Prevention and Treatment Program calls for a 50-game suspension if a player tests positive a first time. The penalty for a second offense is 100 games. If a third offense occurs, the player gets a lifetime ban. All are without pay.

Barry Bonds holds the single-season (73) home run record and passed Hall of Famer Hank Aaron's career mark of 755 with 762. Roger Clemens won 354 games and the seven Cy Young Awards. And then there's Mark McGwire, Sammy Sosa, Rafael Palmeiro, et al. They've all been connected to banned, performance-enhancing substances. They were the great superstars of their era, and yet they've all failed miserably in Hall of Fame voting by the Baseball Writers Association of America.

Ueberroth's 1985 remarks are worth repeating: "Somebody has to say, 'Enough is enough' against drugs. Baseball is going to accomplish this. It's a tiny little segment of society. We're going to remove drugs and be an example."

Like so many others in the fight against drugs he was well-meaning—and naive. While baseball is wonderful in so many ways, it is still just another strata of our society. The problem of drugs reaches everywhere, and baseball is in no way impervious.

3

Owning a Team: How Hard Could It Be?

illie Wilson swung and missed and it was over.

Tug McGraw, fists clenched high above his head, leaped off the Veterans Stadium mound, and the Philadelphia Phillies had beaten Kansas City to win the 1980 World Series.

It had taken 98 years, but the doormats of Major League Baseball finally had a championship to celebrate.

That was October 21, 1980.

Five months later, I sat with Phillies president Ruly Carpenter in his Montchanin, Delaware, living room and tried to figure out why his family, after finally achieving success, was putting the team up for sale.

It was simple, Ruly said.

When Atlanta Braves owner Ted Turner signed the much-traveled, journeyman Claudell Washington to a five-year, $3.5 million contract, Ruly's dad, Bob, and the family said it was time to get out of baseball. In essence, they were waving the white flag.

Ruly Carpenter, who had a deep-rooted passion for the game, kept shaking his head as he talked about the spiraling salaries that free agency had created. The Carpenters, in good conscience, could not remain part of a baseball ownership that continually threw money around so foolishly. They reasoned they couldn't compete against owners willing to spend so freely and unwisely—for mediocre talent.

The Carpenter family's fortune was at risk, they said, if the Phillies tried to compete, or match other owners dollar for dollar.

Selling the team, though, was a stunner. The Carpenters were part of a distinguished fraternity of owners that included Tom Yawkey, Walter O'Malley, Gussie Busch, the Wrigleys, the Griffiths, the Fetzers, et al.

The Phillies, after suffering 51 losing seasons (highlighted by one five-year stretch when they lost more than 100 games each season), after blowing a 6½-game lead and a pennant in 1964, and after being humiliated in League Championship Series play for three consecutive years (1976–78), and having never won a World Series, had finally exorcised those ghosts.

But instead of building on the championship, they sold the team.

"Baseball is changing," said Ruly. "The Wrigley family is selling the Cubs, so we're not alone."

The Phillies, under the same ownership for 38 years, were sold for $30.1 million.

It has amazed me since I began covering Major League Baseball in 1958 that many of the titans of industry, those who run Fortune 500 companies, fail so miserably when they buy into this fraternity.

And how they keep raising the salary bar with mind-boggling signings.

Example: Tom Hicks, whose Texas Rangers had fallen to last in their division in 2000, signed free-agent Alex Rodriguez to the most lucrative contract in sports history: a 10-year deal worth $252 million. The deal was worth $63 million more than the second-richest baseball deal ever.

The move by Hicks prior to the 2001 season was highly criticized at the time for tying up valuable payroll space that could have been spent in improving other areas, such as pitching.

A-Rod, as he became known, remained with the Rangers for just three seasons before he was traded to the Yankees. In each of his years in Texas, the Rangers finished last with a combined record of 216–270.

In 1976, the season before free agency arrived, the average player's salary was $52,300. On Opening Day 2013, the average salary was $3,650,257.

The beloved Gene Autry, one of baseball's richest owners, was also one of the game's biggest spenders. Sadly, the "Cowboy" as he was known, didn't live to see his Angels, in their 42nd year of existence, finally make it to the 2002 World Series and defeat the San Francisco Giants in seven games. Autry, who had owned the Angels since they were added as an expansion team in 1961, died on October 2, 1998, at the age of 91.

On the other hand, owners who've succeeded have learned how to own. Not to meddle, not to micromanage, not to pal around with the hired help. To own, and own only, is the best job description.

According to *Forbes* magazine's annual survey in 2013, the average worth of a major league franchise was $744 million, up 23 percent from the year before.

For the 16th consecutive year, the New York Yankees are the most valuable team at $2.3 billion. The Los Angeles Dodgers were sold to the Guggenheim Partners in 2012 for $2.1 billion after previous owner Frank McCourt had led the storied franchise into bankruptcy.

Even the Miami Marlins, after once again shedding their top players, are worth $520 million.

Shrewd men, who've accumulated millions in their chosen fields, have often said buying a baseball team is not a sound investment, but that's seldom stopped them from joining this select fraternity.

Eddie Robinson, who turned 93 on December 15, 2013, played 13 years (1942–1957) in the major leagues and followed that with front-office positions with six teams; he served as general manager of both the Braves and Rangers. He also worked for the likes of Ted Turner, Eddie Chiles, Charlie Finley, and George Steinbrenner.

To say Eddie got to know most major league owners is putting it mildly.

When he retired in 2004 after 65 years in professional baseball, he'd received paychecks from 16 big-league teams.

Robinson, speaking to me from his home in Fort Worth, Texas, says new owners after a couple of years "have a tendency to think they know how to do it. They've owned the team for two years, have seen what goes on and it looks easy. They say, 'Hell, I can do that.' Those who do that aren't successful.

"Charlie Finley was different. He really could judge people. He was a lot like Billy Beane today. Charlie was an owner who had a good idea about the players."

Eddie worked as farm director for the Kansas City Athletics, under Finley, in the mid-1960s.

It was the Yankees' George Steinbrenner who started the upward wave of high spending for free agents.

I believe once Steinbrenner began signing many of baseball's premier players, public opinion forced the hands of other owners.

Yet despite Steinbrenner's enormous spending, results failed to live up to his payrolls. With checkbook in hand, he continued to lure some of the game's premier players to Yankee Stadium.

When Steinbrenner bought the team in 1973 the Yankees had not been to the World Series since 1964. They corrected that in 1976, but were swept by the Cincinnati Reds. They rebounded to win the championship the next two years, but after 1981, despite Steinbrenner's spending, they went 13 years without an appearance in the postseason.

That changed in 1995 with a postseason trip, and when Hall of Fame skipper Joe Torre took over in 1996, the most productive period in the Steinbrenner reign began.

When I discuss owners getting too involved and not giving their baseball executives a free hand I'm reminded of the press conference the day George Steinbrenner took over. He promised to remain out of the daily affairs of the team. That vow didn't last very long as he became one of the most involved and visible owners in the sport.

George Steinbrenner was not only the face of the Yankees, I cannot remember any team owner as well-known around the world. The Boss became one of the most famous Yankees.

For someone who wasn't going to get involved, he was just the opposite. He became one of the game's most powerful and influential owners. His reign was tumultuous. He battled with other owners and commissioners; he was suspended and fined.

Yet under his command—and that's an understatement—the Yankees won seven World Series, 11 pennants, and became one of the richest franchises in any sport.

Commissioner Bowie Kuhn suspended Steinbrenner in November 1974 for two years—a term later reduced to 15 months—after he pleaded guilty to two charges, one a felony and the other a misdemeanor for making illegal contributions to President Richard Nixon's 1972 re-election campaign.

In July 1990, Commissioner Fay Vincent ordered Steinbrenner to step aside as the Yankees managing general partner for making a $40,000 payment to Howard Spira in an attempt to dig up damaging information about his player Dave Winfield.

By 1990, Steinbrenner had switched managers 18 times and hired 13 general managers.

In fact, Steinbrenner offered Robinson the job of general manager, but Eddie turned it down because he didn't want to move his family and leave Texas.

"I became a special assistant to George for three years," said Robinson. "I scouted some and did some consulting. We had been very friendly up to the point when I went to work for him. It seemed like when you went to work for George your friendship went out the window. It was so strange. He and I were big buddies until I worked for him, even in a lesser capacity. He still got mad at me."

And there have been others too, almost as outrageous as Steinbrenner.

Philip K. Wrigley was enormously successful with his chewing-gum company, but no matter how hard he tried couldn't produce a winner.

He just couldn't get the Chicago Cubs off the ground.

He tried many things, some of them actually hare-brained, but just couldn't land a championship. The last time the Cubs won the National League pennant was 1945, and they haven't won a World Series since 1908.

In an interview years ago, someone asked Wrigley why he remained in baseball.

"Well, there are a lot of reasons," he responded. "I think the team is good for the city and I like the challenge. But when you really get down to it, baseball is too much of a sport to be a business and too much of a business to be a sport."

Another time he wondered out loud how there could be more interest in the Cubs, whom he called a "bunch of clowns" in 1976, than in his very profitable Wrigley Co.

Wrigley liked watching baseball on television better than at Wrigley Field and usually stayed out of the day-to-day operation of the Cubs, unless an All-Star player or manager was involved.

But when Philip K. Wrigley jumped in, controversy usually followed.

In 1935, his first full year as president, the Cubs won the NL pennant. They finished second in 1936 and 1937, then won again in 1938 and 1945. In 1938, Wrigley fired manager Charley Grimm and replaced him with Gabby Hartnett, who directed the team to another pennant. After a hiatus, Grimm returned to the Wrigley Field dugout in 1944 and was the manager when they won their last pennant.

After that, it was mostly downhill, with only some surges under Leo Durocher in the late 1960s and early 1970s.

The late Jerome Holtzman, a close friend who covered Chicago baseball for many years before he died, repeatedly told me that Wrigley was misunderstood.

Holtzman, who was Major League Baseball's official historian, once wrote: "The problem with most baseball fans is that they mistakenly equate good ballclub ownership with the winning of pennants. If a team wins a pennant, the owner is a champion, or so we're told. This is a foolish and erroneous assumption."

Holtzman went on to say, and I disagreed, "the absence of pennants isn't important."

To Jerome, the fact Philip K. Wrigley was "nice to his players, nice to his employees and, most of all, genuinely concerned with the paying public" made him a good owner.

In 1960, Wrigley rehired Grimm as manager, but before the season ended he took Lou Boudreau out of the broadcast booth to replace Grimm and then sent Grimm to the broadcast booth. That didn't work either.

And then there was the "College of Coaches," the most bizarre move Wrigley made as owner of the team.

The plan was to have from eight to 12 managers rotating throughout the Cubs system, with each of them at one time or another becoming the "head coach."

Don Zimmer, who just completed his 65th year in baseball, was in his second season as a player with the Cubs when Wrigley concocted his "College of Coaches."

"There would be no manager with revolving coaches," Zimmer, now senior advisor for the Tampa Bay Rays, told me from his home in Seminole, Florida. "Mr. Wrigley said they'd be going back and forth from our Triple-A club. The theory was that while one of them was serving as head coach, the others would devote their time to teaching the finer points of baseball to the players.

"There was Vedie Himsl, Harry Craft, Elvin Tappe, and Lou Klein. Of that group, only Craft had managed in the majors. That didn't matter to Mr. Wrigley. The idea was to educate us."

Zim said because of the revolving coaches, they wanted to name a team captain.

"And that was me," he said. "Captain of what? On Opening Day, Himsl, the first head coach, made the announcement that the team needed a captain. I laughed; that's when I knew captains were a joke. To me, there was only one captain in baseball and that was the Dodgers' Pee Wee Reese. When I look back, I believe I was chosen because of my work with the young third baseman, Ron Santo. Mr. Wrigley felt the college of coaches needed a veteran 'assistant' on the field."

In his 2001 book *Zim*, written with Bill Madden, Zimmer said: "I suppose I should have been honored—after all, Ernie Banks was on this team—but when you're a lifetime .235 hitter, being a captain doesn't mean a whole helluva lot.

"Nevertheless, I quickly found out the captaincy had its advantages. Not long after Himsl informed me of the front office's decision, I called Pee Wee and asked him if being the captain was worth any extra money. Much to my surprise, he told me the Dodgers gave him an extra $500 every year he was captain.

"Well, when the first paychecks arrived that season, I discovered an extra check with mine for $500. Suddenly, I started having a different outlook about being captain. It might be a crock, but at least it was a worthwhile crock. Fifteen days later, the next check came and, much to my surprise, there was another check for $500. I figured this had to be a mistake, but I didn't say anything.

"Then, two weeks later, I got another $500 check with my regular check and now I was worried. I didn't want to have them come to me at the end of the season and say they'd made a mistake and that I owed them all that money—or that I had to pay extra taxes on all those captain's checks. So, I went to John Holland, the general manager, and told him I thought there was a mistake. He said, 'Mr. Wrigley wants it this way as long as you're doing your job with the young players.'"

Lou Boudreau, who replaced Charley Grimm during the second half of the 1960 season, was fired and sent to the radio booth.

"The last day of the season he was waiting for me to do a radio interview," Zimmer remembered. "I loved Chicago and the Cubs treated me well, but there was no way that I wanted to continue under those circumstances. Charley Grimm is sitting by the dugout and he's hearing the show on the radio. Boudreau asked me if I thought it [college of coaches] worked. I said, 'Yeah. We lost a hundred games [actually 90]. It worked.' I said, 'The Cubs have been wonderful to me, but I'd prefer to go elsewhere if possible. One manager is enough.'"

Zimmer said the plan started on Opening Day in Cincinnati, with Himsl the head coach.

"I played for Himsl and Craft, and all of a sudden Lou Klein comes in as the third head coach. I said, 'I ain't playing.'"

He added, "I guess this has happened before, but the moment the season was over, the season in which I was named team captain and an All-Star, the Cubs got rid of me."

The College of Coaches notwithstanding, Zim had nothing but kind words about Wrigley.

"Of all the owners I worked for, he was one I never met," he said. "I just never met the guy."

Zimmer returned to the Cubs as manager for four seasons beginning in 1988. In 1989, his team won the division title, but didn't advance past the NL Championship Series. He was voted NL Manager of the Year that season.

Wrigley died at age 82 on April 12, 1977. On February 11 of that year, in one of his last baseball moves, he traded two-time National League batting champion Bill Madlock to the San Francisco Giants. Wrigley said he dealt Madlock rather than submit to what he considered exorbitant salary demands. Madlock, who batted .354 in 1975 and .339 the following season, was earning just $80,000 before he was traded.

The Wrigley era ended in 1981 when the family sold the team to the Tribune Company.

Wrigley was one of the first owners to stop the practice of selling advertising billboards on the outfield walls and instead covered Wrigley Field's outfield walls with ivy.

More important, he adamantly refused to install lights for night baseball. He said it wasn't fair to the residents whose homes ring the ballpark on the North Side.

But after the Tribune Company purchased the team—and ballpark—and Dallas Green became general manager in 1982, he maintained the Cubs could not be competitive without night baseball. It took a number of years, but even though Green left in 1987, lights were installed in 1988.

———•———

The Texas Rangers ownership debacle actually began in our nation's capital.

Late in 1968, Robert E. (Bob) Short purchased the struggling Washington Senators, a 1961 expansion team.

Short, a self-made millionaire through the successful operation of trucking, hotel, and legal businesses, craved ownership of sports franchises. He was usually able to use funds provided by others to finance his sports projects.

Bob Short paid $10 million for the Senators and brought in Ted Williams as manager.

From the outset, Short had financial problems and was forced to sell his best players to pay his bills. He blasted Washington fans for lack of support and in 1972 moved the Senators to Arlington, Texas, where they became the Rangers.

He described himself as "probably the most unpopular man in Washington."

Before Short left our nation's capital without a major league team he lashed out at then Commissioner Bowie Kuhn.

In Kuhn's 1987 memoir *Hardball: The Education of a Baseball Commissioner*, this passage defines the type of owner Short was. "Both attendance and the ballclub slumped in 1970, dooming Washington in Short's eyes," Kuhn wrote. "By early April 1971, Short made it clear to me in a long, rambling, emotional late-night telephone conversation that he was not staying in Washington.

"'No one can keep me in Washington, not Nixon, not Cronin [American League president Joe Cronin], not Kuhn. I will cannibalize the club if necessary. I own it and I will take it to St. Paul if I want. I have lawyers too. I will move wherever I want. Congress will not help me because of your position. I don't give a goddamn if they stick you with the antitrust laws. I'll go to St. Paul, Dallas, or Toronto. [Arthur] Goldberg is my lawyer and I'll go the whole goddamn distance with you. Hoffberger [Orioles owner Jerry Hoffberger]] is a genius. Let him figure it out. Or let Walter O'Malley and his National League friends help out.

"'No place in Washington is safe at night and Nixon can't do anything about it. I may sell Ted Williams to Boston or Knowles, or Howard, or Epstein. Ted says Washington is a horseshit town and I've gotta get out. I'll go elsewhere before I'm forced into bankruptcy like Seattle. I know I had my eyes wide open when I went to Washington, everybody has to give something: me, the players, the TV, and the federal government. Even the Humphrey Democrats are now hitting me. Maybe things will work out in a Cinderella way, but that's not likely.'"

Kuhn then wrote, beautifully summing up Bob Short, who died in 1982: "That monologue perfectly catches the essence of Short and his wild, flailing style, his penchant for lashing out at everybody. There was little doubt in my mind that his goal was Arlington, Texas, between Dallas and Fort Worth."

And then there was Brad Corbett, who made his millions in the plastics industry and rescued the financially failing Short when he bought the Rangers in the spring of 1974.

He was another of the owners who tried to buy a championship. Corbett was one of the most active owners when free agency became a way of life in major league baseball.

He lured Doyle Alexander away from the Yankees for $750,000; he signed Doc Medich for $1 million and promised him another $50,000 a year to be a Rangers physician if and when Medich's arm was worn out. Corbett gave slugger Richie Zisk a 10-year, $2.96 million contract to leave the White Sox.

There was Campy Campaneris getting $1 million and Bert Blyleven getting a lucrative extension that was to last until 2000. But he was then traded to the Pittsburgh Pirates.

Corbett, the owner, was deeply involved in the team.

Eddie Robinson, who'd been the Atlanta Braves general manager since 1972—it was Eddie who traded Hank Aaron to the Brewers on November 2, 1974, so he could finish his career in Milwaukee, where it began in 1954—became Rangers GM after the 1976 season.

Ted Turner had purchased the Braves earlier in 1976 and kept Robinson on as his general manager, but when Corbett offered

Eddie an opportunity to return to his native Texas he jumped at the chance.

Robinson's first season with the Rangers was tumultuous to say the least. There was Lenny Randle's attack on manager Frank Lucchesi during Spring Training. In June, the team was floundering. Corbett and Robinson fired Lucchesi and hired Eddie Stanky, who quit after only one game. Billy Hunter eventually replaced Stanky, who finished the season with a 60–33 record and held the division lead as late as August 19. Kansas City took the division with 102 victories.

"Brad was a great guy, a great boss, but a loose cannon," said Robinson. "He loved to make trades, talk trades. Many's the time he'd wake me up at two o'clock in the morning to ask me about a trade he'd thought of."

Eddie Robinson's years with the Rangers included five managerial changes.

Corbett, who died in 2012, was mired in red ink in 1980 when he was rescued by Eddie Chiles of Fort Worth, owner of the Western Company, a worldwide oil-field supply firm.

As for Corbett, reporter Randy Galloway wrote: "'It's a case of mismanagement at the worst,' an American League official said."

Don Zimmer was Rangers manager for the 1981 and 1982 seasons.

"That was a joke," Zimmer told me.

"I could sit down for an hour and you wouldn't believe some of the things I could tell you. Eddie Robinson was a good baseball man, but he was scared to death of Eddie Chiles, who was so strong in his mind.

"Eddie called me in one day and said this is what Chiles wants. He wants you to sit down with every player and ask him how many home runs he's going to hit the rest of the year [and] what his batting average is going to be the rest of the year.

"The first guy I called in was Buddy Bell, our best player. I said, 'Buddy, how many home runs do you think you're going to hit the rest of the year?' Buddy looked at me and said, 'How the hell do I know?' I told him that's the answer I thought I'd get.

Then, Leon Roberts came in and I asked him the same question. He wasn't even playing, but said 20 home runs. After asking a handful of guys, I just threw all the paper in the garbage can. I said if this is what managing is about, I don't want to be here.

"That's the only place I ever managed where I was glad I was fired because of the circumstances."

Zimmer likes to tell the story the first day he met Eddie Chiles in a Dallas hotel suite after being hired as manager in December 1980.

"'Mr. Manager,' he said in a commanding tone. 'This is directed at you.'

"He started, 'I'm a very successful oilman. I started out from scratch, with nothing, and founded the Western Oil Company of North America in 1939. I started out with three employees, two trucks and $10,000 in debt, and built the company into a $500 million corporation with 5,000 employees. I did it despite the government continually trying to interfere in my business. I don't really like baseball the way it is now. I think it needs a lot of improvements, but I'm gonna run my baseball team the way I run my oil company.

"'Now, you're getting top dollar to be my manager, and as such, you will live in the Metroplex area like all of my other employees.'"

Zimmer says he asked Chiles what the Metroplex was and was told in no uncertain terms he'd be required to live there full-time.

"That's when I got up, complimented him on his achievements and said, 'I'm sure you probably have some good ideas on how to improve baseball, but as of right now, the one thing you don't have is a manager.'"

As Zimmer walked out of the room, Chiles stopped him, reneged, and allowed him to keep his permanent residence in Florida.

Another Zimmer story from his days managing for Chiles: "Randy Galloway, the writer, and our wives were driving to Louisiana on an off-day to the horse races. During the trip, I said to Randy, 'For some reason I've got a sneaky suspicion I'm going to get fired today.' When we pulled up at the track, a security officer said, 'Are you Don Zimmer?' I said, 'Yes, sir.' He told me Mr. Chiles had called and wanted me to call him right away. I said to Randy, 'Let's go play the daily double first and then I'll call him.'

"We got the women settled, bet the double, and I called one of Eddie Chiles' right-hand men. He said Mr. Chiles wants to send his plane over and get you right back because he wants to have a press conference tonight. The women drove the cars home and Randy and I took Chiles' plane back. When we got back there, the press conference was going to be in a few minutes.

"It wasn't me; I got saved. Eddie Robinson was fired.

"The next day Mr. Chiles called me into his office over at Fort Worth. He was like a Steinbrenner in a way. He said, 'As of today, every trade, everything we do is going to have your okay. After that, it's your team. I said to myself, 'I just got big!' I told him, 'I'll go along with that.'

"We went on a four-day road trip and when we got back, I got a phone call to be in Eddie Chiles' office at nine o'clock tomorrow morning. He told me, 'We're going to make a managerial change.' I had made no changes, had no say on anything, I never got a chance; I was six-foot-six for about five minutes.

"I'm fired, but then he says, 'I want you to manage the club for the next three days.' I go into the dugout the next game and about the third inning the clubhouse man came to me and said, 'I hear you got fired.' There was only one person who could have leaked it out: Eddie Chiles."

Zimmer added, "That night and the next day, when I went out to home plate with the lineup card, I got a standing ovation, but I was fired. Everybody said I was nuts, but I said, 'I'm getting paid. What am I supposed to do?'"

Chiles, who died in 1993, publicly chastised Kuhn for his mishandling of the 50-day players' strike in 1981. The next year he cast a critical vote that began the process to remove Kuhn from office.

With mounting losses in the oil business, he sold the Rangers to a group headed by George W. Bush in March 1989.

The future governor of Texas and president of the United States and his ownership group finally brought stability to the franchise.

Baseball was never the same after Charlie Finley bought the Kansas City Athletics in December 1960. He was a maverick, a renegade owner.

In 1963, Finley changed the Athletics' home-white and road-gray uniforms into Kelly green, "Fort Knox" gold, and white. In 1967, he replaced their traditional black baseball cleats with white ones. He also phased out Athletics on the uniforms with A's.

According to *Baseball Digest*, when Mickey Mantle first saw the new green, gold, and white uniforms, he said, "They should come out of the dugout on tippy-toes, holding hands and singing."

Eddie Robinson became Finley's assistant general manager in 1966, working with GM Eddie Lopat. Lopat has the title, but Charlie O. was always his own general manager.

"He was somewhat distant, but liked to control things—and did," Robinson told me during a 2013 interview. "He had a lot of ideas, some of them damn good, which are still followed today."

Eight years after buying the A's, Finley moved them to Oakland.

Unlike many new owners, almost from his first days in Kansas City, he built a strong farm system and amassed players such as Reggie Jackson, Sal Bando, Joe Rudi, Bert Campaneris, Catfish Hunter, Rollie Fingers, and Vida Blue.

I began to follow and report on the A's in the early 1970s as they became postseason regulars. They won three straight World Series from 1972 to 1974 and five straight division titles from 1971 to 1975 in the Oakland Coliseum, where they still play.

Once, during a World Series, I was granted a sit-down interview with Finley. It was supposed to last just 10 minutes. We spoke for 90 minutes, and by the time he finished telling me all the innovations that would help baseball my head was spinning, and later my editors were shaking their heads as well.

I asked him why he, the owner, did not have a general manager.

"When the day comes that I find a GM who can do a better job than Charlie O., I'll hire the son-of-a-gun," he said with a twinge of arrogance.

He seemed to always be bubbling over with new ideas—like the orange baseballs he tried in a few exhibition games in 1973, or offering $300 bonuses to players to grow moustaches during the championships. That's when relief pitcher Rollie Fingers grew his handlebar number, which he has kept to this day—his trademark.

Finley lost Hunter—Charlie nicknamed him "Catfish" to garner attention from the media—to free agency over the details of how a $50,000 insurance annuity would be handled. The two disagreed and when the players union filed a grievance seeking free agency on the basis Finley failed to make the payment, arbitrator Peter Seitz ruled in favor of Hunter.

Hunter was a prize. He'd won 20 or more games four consecutive years for the A's, with a 25–12 record and 2.49 earned run average his last season there. He was 4–0 in World Series games and was the 1974 AL Cy Young Award winner.

That was the winter of 1974. I remember most of the major league teams sending representatives to Hunter's home in Ahoskie, North Carolina, trying to persuade him to sign. A Who's Who in Baseball knocked on his door. The Yankees finally landed Hunter with a contract that had a total estimated value of $3.5 million.

He was 23–14, with a 2.58 ERA in 1975, his first of five years with the Yankees.

The Yankees won three straight pennants (1976–78) with Hunter, who was elected to the Hall of Fame in 1987.

Yankees owner George Steinbrenner once said, "Catfish Hunter was the cornerstone of the Yankees' success over the last quarter of a century. We were not winning before he arrived."

Finley started dismantling the A's after Hunter left. He attempted to sell Rudi and Fingers to the Red Sox and Blue to the Yankees.

In a highly publicized move, Kuhn put up the stop sign, invoking the "best interests of baseball" clause to void the sales. Finley took him to court and lost the case.

Finley eventually lost most of those players to free agency anyway.

Facing a divorce that would make it impossible to keep the team, Finley sold the team to Walter A. Haas before the start of the 1981 season.

Eddie Robinson's favorite Charlie Finley story revolved around the Rangers' purchase of left-handed relief pitcher Paul Lindblad on February 19, 1977.

"We acquired him from the A's for $400,000," remembered Robinson. "The commissioner, Bowie Kuhn, jumped up in the air about it. A hearing was held in Dallas and after that the commissioner established 'The Lindblad Rule.' No team could sell a player for more than $400,000."

Kuhn said, "I decided to make that the ceiling price for all major league player sales."

After his year with Finley in Kansas City, Robinson followed his mentor, Paul Richards, to Atlanta as the Braves' farm director. Four years later, in 1972, the Braves elevated him to general manager, a post he held until he returned home to work with the Rangers.

Ted Turner is more the exception than the rule when it comes to major league owners.

In the beginning, "The Mouth of the South," was out of control when he purchased the Braves in 1976.

He was a thorn in Bowie Kuhn's side.

Consider:

- He put on the uniform and managed the Braves in one game until the commissioner told him he couldn't do that. As a manager, Ted opened and closed in one game.
- He hung the legend "Channel 17" on the back of Andy Messersmith's uniform as an ad for his fledgling cable superstation.
- He tampered with free-agent outfielder Gary Matthews and got suspended for it.
- He was the first owner to charge the press to eat in the media dining room.

But then, something came over Ted Turner. For whatever reason, and this is often so difficult for ego-driven owners to do, he retreated and turned over operation of his sports empire (he also owned the NBA Atlanta Hawks) to capable sports executives such as Stan Kasten and John Schuerholz. He learned to trust their advice.

With the Braves in a no-end-in-sight losing streak, Dave Bristol was away on a Turner-imposed vacation. So, Ted tried to manage the Braves as a temporary replacement. Kuhn and National League president Chub Feeney "fired" him after one game. They ruled anyone who owned stock in a club couldn't manage it.

To that, I remember Turner's comment: "They must have put that rule in yesterday. If I'm smart enough to save up $11 million to buy the team, I ought to be smart enough to manage it."

Then, with a belly laugh, he added: "Managing isn't that difficult. All you have to do is score more runs than the other guy!"

The game was at Pittsburgh's Three Rivers Stadium on May 11, 1977—Turner's second season as owner. He was 38 years old.

He wore uniform No. 27 and sat quietly in the dugout as the Braves lost to the Pirates 2–1 for their 17th consecutive defeat. They lost 101 games that dreadful summer.

He said he originally had planned to manage his team for 10 days while Bristol relaxed at his North Carolina home. Kuhn and Feeney had other ideas.

"I want to manage even more now because they don't want me to," Turner said. "Everybody in baseball takes this all too seriously. This is just like a big Little League team to me."

A year later, in a *Playboy* interview, a more serious Turner said: "I figured if I could just get down in the dugout with some authority, I might find out what was wrong. When things are going bad, there are 10,000 guys in the stands who think, 'If I could just take over this ballclub for a while, I'd straighten them out.' But Bowie Kuhn said I couldn't manage again. I asked him if it was okay if I went and managed in the minors for a year and really learned how to do it. He said, 'Nope.'"

"Ted was really a good guy," said Robinson. "He had never been around baseball and didn't know baseball. He did some things people didn't understand, but knowing his 'rookie' status, I could understand it. He and I got along fine.

"He learned, and I think that is the point that has to be made about him."

In the late 1980s and early '90s, I co-hosted a Saturday baseball show on Turner's CNN cable network. Because I was in Atlanta so often, I'd often have a chance to chat briefly with Ted.

Once, as delicately as I could word it, I mentioned the Carpenters leaving baseball because they were irritated with his signing of Claudell Washington. He never answered, but as he walked away I think I saw a smile on his face.

If he could stir the pot, Ted Turner was in his element.

———

I sat with Ray Kroc at an owners meeting soon after he bought the San Diego Padres in January 1974.

There was a catching spirit-lifting jingle in the McDonald's TV ads that year—fast-moving lyrics about the contents of the Big Mac.

"Two all-beef patties, lettuce, cheese, pickles, onions, special sauce on a sesame seed bun—the Big Mac!"

Now shouldn't the founder of the hamburger chain be able to recite the jingle?

"I'm very sorry to tell you I cannot say it because it goes too fast," he said.

I remember leading my column that day with Kroc's inability to repeat the ditty about his most popular product.

The follow-up paragraph was about how in January 1974 at the proverbial 11th hour he bought the Padres and saved baseball in San Diego.

I attended the owners meeting that year when it was a given the Padres were being transferred to Washington.

Then, as if riding in on a white horse, feisty Ray Kroc saved the franchise—a Cubs fan who grew up in Chicago, following the likes of Hack Wilson, Gabby Hartnett, Rogers Hornsby, Stan Hack, Phil Cavarretta, et al. But his strong interest in baseball led him to buy the Padres and eventually move his home to San Diego. He pumped money into the franchise and made it successful.

Dave Anderson, Pulitzer Prize–winning sports columnist for the *New York Times*, wrote this about Kroc's entry into baseball:

During the Padres' opener in San Francisco after Kroc purchased the team in 1974, he and general manager Buzzy Bavasi were sitting together "when their left fielder, Nate Colbert, butchered a ball. The misplay enabled the Giants to take a quick lead. Ray Kroc bristled.

"'Get rid of him,' the owner said. 'I want you to get rid of him immediately.'

"But in the eighth inning, Nate Colbert hit a home run that would win the game. Ray Kroc was on his feet, applauding, but Buzzy Bavasi stayed in his seat.

"'What's the matter, Buzzy?' the owner asked. 'Why aren't you clapping for Nate's homer?'

"'That can't be Colbert,' his GM said. 'I had to get rid of him, remember?'"

Later that year at the Padres home opener, they were losing to the Astros 9–5, when their leadoff hitter walked in the ninth inning. Manager John McNamara inserted a pinch runner, but before the next pitch, he was picked off first base.

Ray Kroc jumped up from his seat and hurried to the public-address announcer's booth. He commandeered the microphone and identified himself to the fans at San Diego Stadium as the team owner.

"I suffer with you," he started to say to the spectators.

Just then, a streaker ran across the outfield.

"Get that streaker!" Ray Kroc barked into the microphone, then paused while his order was obeyed.

Later, he continued with the fans.

"I have some good news and some bad news," he said. "The good news is that we've outdrawn the Dodgers. They had 31,000 for their opener and we have 39,000. The bad news is that I've never seen such stupid ballplaying in my life."

Like Ted Turner, Ray Kroc had to learn about baseball the hard way. And about Bowie Kuhn and National League president Chub Feeney.

Ray was enthusiastic and dynamic. But when he made impetuous remarks about coveting Yankees third baseman Graig Nettles and Cincinnati Reds second baseman Joe Morgan, Kuhn slapped him with a $100,000 fine and charged him with tampering.

"There's a lot more future in hamburgers than baseball," Kroc, 76 at the time, said. "The fun is all over for me. Baseball isn't baseball anymore. It's brought me nothing but aggravation."

Kroc had owned the team for six years, but turned the day-to-day operation over to his son-in-law Ballard Smith.

Ray Kroc died January 14, 1984, at the age of 81.

The bottom line is if many of these millionaires had operated their businesses the way they did their baseball teams, they never would have made the millions with which they bought their teams.

"My experiences in Texas back that up," said Zimmer. "You cannot say that about all of them. When it comes to owners like Walter O'Malley and Tom Yawkey, they were special, tremendous. They helped make the game as great as it is.

"I got very close to Mr. Yawkey. I was just a coach and he knew I came to the ballpark early. He would be sitting in my chair, waiting for me to get there at three o'clock in the afternoon, just to talk baseball with me. He was a wonderful man.

"And I never heard a bad word about Gene Autry. He just never got lucky."

4

Bill Clinton and the Strike of '94

Outside, a bitter February freeze swept through Washington's evening hours and chilled thoughts of the summer game.

Inside, a roaring fire did little to warm the frozen cold war between baseball players and Major League owners this wintry night in 1995.

It was a typical February day in Washington—cold, cloudy, depressing.

Spring Training was just nine days away and here we were at the White House, with the president of the United States trying desperately to end a players' strike that had silenced the game since August 12, 1994.

The 1994 World Series had fallen victim to the dispute, hundreds of games had been canceled, and now the '95 season was in jeopardy.

It was February 7, 1995, and in a last-ditch attempt Bill Clinton had gathered negotiators from both sides to the White House, threatening them with a deadline to reach an agreement.

In a sense, this was a national crisis, even though the combatants didn't convene on this sub-freezing day in the stealthy atmosphere of the White House Situation Room.

But nevertheless, the parties were summoned to 1600 Pennsylvania Avenue, arguably the most famous address in the world. Stately, historic rooms in the West Wing, not too far from the Oval Office, were the scene.

A crackling fire burned in a fireplace at the end of the legendary Roosevelt Room, warming the otherwise chilly atmosphere, while a large grandfather clock a few feet away ticked off the long hours of what became an exhausting day.

Above the mantel hung the famed *Rough Rider* portrait, showing Teddy Roosevelt on horseback and when several of the players leading negotiations for their side arrived, Clinton, jacket off, shirtsleeves rolled up, walked through the adjacent large mahogany door from the Oval Office.

"He immediately pointed to the portrait and started to give us a history of the Bully Pulpit," remembered David Cone, the former pitcher who was the American League player representative in 1995. "He said, 'I don't really have any power here except the Bully Pulpit.' He then explained how it works and what he was trying to do that night."

"Bully Pulpit" was coined by President Teddy Roosevelt, referring to the White House, by which he meant a terrific platform from which to advocate an agenda. Clinton was trying to use the power of that "bully pulpit" to get our national pastime back on the field.

"He made us feel very welcome that night—warm, very engaging," said Cone, who had earned the AL Cy Young Award from the strike year. Now a Yankees broadcaster, he won 194 games while pitching for five teams during a 17-year career, which included a perfect game in 1999.

"We expressed our opinions and concerns on the matter," said pitcher Tom Glavine, then an All-Star left-hander with the Atlanta Braves and recently elected to the Hall of Fame. "We didn't want to send a letter to him from our lawyers. We wanted it to be from the players. We didn't ask for anything; we didn't demand anything."

I remember the atmosphere as somber and serious, yet with an almost festive twinge. The players, obviously unaccustomed to the surrounds steeped with so much history, seemed almost giddy at times.

Secret Service agents and other White House staffers directed them to be seated at the long table that occupies most of the space in the Roosevelt Room.

"I was humbled being there," said former pitcher Scott Sanderson, then a member of the union's executive council. "I took it [being at the White House] very seriously. We realized we're just a game of baseball and there were a lot more important things going on in the world. I didn't want to overplay our importance of being there.

"The fact that we were sitting at the table in the Roosevelt Room and just to think about the meetings that had taken place there which had [an] impact on the world was eerie. And we were sitting at that same table, having discussions. The moment certainly wasn't lost on me."

Early in the afternoon, I walked up the driveway leading to the West Wing with Interim Commissioner Bud Selig. His face was drawn, and with a frown he said, "We're in for a long day."

Selig had been appointed chairman of Major League Baseball's governing executive council on September 9, 1992, following Fay Vincent's forced resignation. He was essentially the interim commissioner before being elected full-time to the prestigious position on July 9, 1998—baseball's ninth commissioner. He has been in office ever since, presiding over enormous growth and changes in the sport.

"It was a very emotional day and again it proved how really important baseball is to America and society," Selig remembers. "When you have the president of the United States involved it says everything.

"The press coverage was unbelievable. My wife was in Israel that night and saw me on television walking out of the White House."

I remember the grueling hours of waiting, almost breathlessly hoping Clinton would emerge with an announcement, not short of "Play ball!"

As outside temperatures plummeted to the 20s, Clinton-aide George Stephanopoulos was busy keeping the fire going in the Roosevelt Room, fetching oak logs and hurling them on the flames as sparks flew.

"It was an unusual time," Stephanopoulos, now co-host of ABC's *Good Morning America,* recalled with a laugh. "We'd just gotten our clocks cleaned with the mid-term elections, it was the first time [for Clinton] with the Republican majority in the House, and the possibility of whether Colin Powell was going to be challenging. There was all this stuff going on and yet a day was spent trying to solve the baseball problem."

Maybe a tad naïve about how grounded the two sides were, Clinton beseeched, if not ordered players and owners "to give us back our pastime."

"The thought that crossed my mind was that the president of the United States had the business and responsibility of running the country and that wasn't going to be put on hold because baseball had a hiccup," said Sanderson.

Sanderson found it interesting that Clinton, Vice President Al Gore, and the administration "in the 11th hour [of the strike] could come in and thought they could have a significant impact on basically the history of where we were at that stage and how we could move forward. Really, the most they could do was to implore us to do what was in the best interest for the game of baseball and the entertainment value it provided to the people of this country.

"Actually, there wasn't a whole lot more that was going to get accomplished other than the administration putting forward their feelings and desires—that we find a resolution."

Chances of a settlement early in 1994, as the season opened with the former collective bargaining agreement expired, became hopeless when management's proposal centered around a salary cap. There was little hope the players union would ever agree to anything that limited salary growth.

The president's suit was dark brown, his shirt starched white, his tie a darker brown, his mood just as dark when he surfaced as the clock inched toward 11:00 PM.

"They are clearly not capable of settling this strike without an umpire," a somber and weary Clinton said after more than six hours of failed negotiations. "I have done all I can do to change this situation."

Baseball is more than a sport. It's a national treasure, a valuable resource that had been taken away.

"It was a heartbreaking, terrible story," said Selig as he looks back. "We had lost the World Series and now the 1995 season was in danger. You have reminders like this how important baseball really is."

Selig remembers the players walking around the Roosevelt Room and other areas of the White House.

"In a sense, in a lot of ways, it was a bizarre scene," he said. "But here we were in the White House. I spent a lot of time alone with the president, as did a lot of other people."

Clinton, who talked with me about being an avid Cardinals fan and listening to their broadcasts while growing up in Arkansas, believed it would be in the best interests of everyone if players and team owners could settle their dispute themselves.

He was adamant, however, that the strike had left baseball with a "tarnished image," and added that the dispute "was trying the patience and depressing the spirits of millions of baseball fans—including me."

The verbal firing continued when Labor Secretary Robert Reich said, "On this the 100th anniversary of Babe Ruth's birth, the Babe would not be enormously optimistic for any quick settlement."

Fans across America were depressed, disgusted, and angered.

Off the fields, thousands of jobs were imperiled. Tens of thousands of workers whose jobs depended on baseball were huge losers, as what would become the longest strike in professional sports continued.

It reached deep into our society. It is a game that has created untold jobs and revenue—from the concession operators to ticket

takers to grounds crews to all the licensed merchandise that is sold. And then there is the tax revenue generated from all of the above, not to mention taxes the teams and players themselves pay.

The players believed a third-party solution had a chance to be closer to the proposals owners repeatedly rejected. They wanted Clinton to hear their views as directly as possible.

"They took a heckuva shot that night to try to settle the issues. That's why it went on and on and why we stayed there for such a long time," said Cone. "President Clinton was in and out of our sessions, trying to balance this with other pressing issues.

"Al Gore seemed to take the lead, and Stephanopoulos facilitated the individual meetings—two on twos, three on threes, breaking groups down trying to get things done. George was working the mechanism behind the scenes."

Stephanopoulos said, "I wasn't a negotiator, just one of the White House representatives trying to facilitate the sessions more than anything else."

Pausing and staring off into space, Cone said, "I almost felt embarrassed, telling the president, 'We've taken up too much of your time.'"

Once, Clinton walked by and quipped, "It's just a few hundred folks trying to figure out how to divide nearly $2 billion. They ought to be able to figure that out."

Yes, it was the biggest strike ever in professional sports.

While reporting for *USA TODAY,* I wrote that this had become nothing more than a fierce battle of the Hatfields and McCoys.

The union, i.e., the Major League Players Association, had become the strongest and wealthiest union on the planet.

The powerful players association was led by Don Fehr, highly intelligent, pragmatic, and often emotionless. He's one of the best labor lawyers in America and continued the rigid stance of the players established by the late Marvin Miller, the MLBPA's first executive director.

Fehr led the baseball union for 26 years (1983–2009) through collusion cases and a long list of labor battles. He's now executive director of the National Hockey League Players Association, and in 2012–13 guided that union through a bitter owners' lockout. With that, he became the only executive director of a players union to be directly involved in work stoppages in two sports.

Six of the eight contract negotiations he has been involved in have resulted in work stoppages, including five consecutive negotiations between baseball players and owners.

"President Clinton remarked to me that night in 1995 how united our players were," said Fehr.

"He said the same thing to us," Cone remembered. "He said, 'I admire you guys for hanging together.'"

The day/night at the White House became so important because on January 26 players and owners were ordered by Clinton to resume bargaining (talks had earlier broken off) and to reach an agreement by February 6. The deadline came and went with no resolution, prompting Clinton to extend the deadline by a day. Five days earlier, the owners had agreed to revoke their demand of a salary cap and return to the old CBA.

"I had hoped that tonight I'd be telling you that baseball would be coming back in 1995," Clinton said when the sessions finally ended. "And for a good while this evening I thought that might well be the case. Unfortunately, the parties have not reached agreement. The American people are the real losers.

"The major league cities, the Spring Training communities, the families of thousands of Americans who won't have work unless there's a baseball season are the losers. And, of course, the millions of fans who have waited for six long months for the owners and players to give us back our national pastime."

Clinton added that because "I have no legal authority in this situation I will send legislation to Congress seeking binding arbitration of the baseball dispute. This is not a request for a congressionally imposed solution. It is a request for the only process we have left to find a solution through neutral parties. The only way to do this appears to be for Congress to step up to the plate and pass the legislation."

Congress, of course, had more pressing business, but Americans and baseball fans considered the strike just as pressing.

"There *is* something the American people can do," Clinton, his voice hoarse, said. "They can tell their senator or representative whether they feel this is a proper case for binding arbitration."

Then, with a pained look, he said, "Last fall, for the first time in 90 years, there was no World Series. When something goes on for that long without interruption, seeing our nation through wars, dramatic social changes, it becomes more than a game, more than simply a way to pass time. It becomes part of who we are. We've all got to work to preserve that part.

"I call on the players and the owners to go back, keep talking, and work through this."

Selig took responsibility for calling off the postseason and World Series and it will be a large footnote to his legacy.

Truly, it's a bum rap. He had no other choice.

"I didn't call it off; the players were on strike," Selig said 20 years later. "I remember Sal Bando and Phil Garner coming into my office saying, 'These guys are out of shape, they cannot play.' We didn't have a deal anyway."

In 1904, there was no World Series between the American League champion Boston Red Sox and the National League champion New York Giants. Owing to a business rivalry between the two leagues, especially in New York, and to personal animosity between Giants manager John McGraw and AL president Ban Johnson, the Giants declined to meet the champions of the "junior" or "minor" league. McGraw insisted his Giants were already the world champions since they were the champions of the "only real major league."

The strike was baseball's eighth work stoppage since 1972. The final 52 days and 669 games of the 1994 season, plus the World Series and playoffs, had been canceled.

All of which led to the long day of negotiations at the White House on February 7, 1995. Clinton demanded the sides agree to binding arbitration, which would become the theme of the evening.

"At one point I thought we'd break through, but it fell apart at the end," remembers Cone. "The final issue was—the owners would do binding arbitration on just one issue—the cost of labor or the salary-cap issue. Don Fehr said if we're going to do binding arbitration we're going to do the whole thing. Bud Selig wanted to carve it out.

"It was a long day that ended very badly. We were all upset. We thought we were going to get something done there and it just didn't happen."

In 1992, major league owners forced Commissioner Fay Vincent to resign. He had irritated them with some of his previous actions, but most of all the owners, led by Selig (then owner of the Milwaukee Brewers), didn't want Vincent to interfere with negotiations as the current CBA was expiring.

There had been a strike or lockout every time the CBA had previously expired. Richard Ravitch was hired at a salary greater than Vincent's to negotiate a new deal, the core of which was the salary cap. The players association was vehemently opposed to this.

The strike began on August 12. On-and-off negotiations continued. When it became obvious there would be no agreement, Selig, the interim commissioner, called off the postseason and World Series on September 14, 1994.

Ravitch was ultimately replaced as the saga continued into the winter. Owners used several different lead negotiators while the union's leadership remained intact.

A concerned Clinton, demonstrating how important baseball is to America, appointed Willie J. Usery Jr., former labor secretary, to mediate the dispute.

The bickering, the rhetoric, the accusations, it became a cathartic event.

When Clinton, playing his own version of hardball, originally gave owners and players 24 hours to make a deal, he summoned Bill Usery to the White House.

"I have never before in my life been given as strong a request to do my utmost in reaching a settlement," the sometimes avuncular Usery said. "The president told me I must get it done by five o'clock Monday [February 6]."

There was no settlement. Monday turned into Tuesday and by noon Clinton was irritated. Negotiators were already meeting in a Washington hotel, so logistics weren't a problem when he notified them to come to the White House.

"We were in Washington for so many weeks. We were lobbying Congress on the antitrust issue. And nobody had any clothes left," said Cone. "I had a couple of suits, so I put on a suit for the White House. Tommy Glavine and some of the others—they didn't have clothes suitable for the White House. They ended up wearing khakis and no socks."

Laughing, Cone added, "They got killed. The *New York Times* took a picture of us walking into the White House wearing sweaters, khakis, polo shirts, and no socks!"

As the night wore on, the players wandered around the White House. During an interlude, Glavine worked with the president on his golf swing. Those were the lighter moments. Clinton obviously enjoyed being around the players and even went to lengths to discuss his own athletic prowess.

The president of the United States, the most powerful man in the free world, working on his golf swing with instruction from a ballplayer.

"It was very casual," said Cone. "President Clinton was intensely interested in golf and knew several of the players were very good at it.

"I remember talking to him about Diet Cokes—he was drinking a Diet Coke—and how this is bad for us. He made us all feel very welcome that night. We had a lot of one-on-one time with him. I'm repeating myself, but I don't care what your politics are, he has that warmth about him. He has this gift of making people feel welcome."

Spring Training obviously didn't begin on time.

On March 28, the players voted to return to the field if a U.S. District Court judge supported the National Labor Relations Board's unfair labor practices complaint, which had been lodged against the owners, who the day before had voted to use replacement players.

Future Supreme Court justice Sonia Sotomayor heard the case on a hot March day in a crowded New York courtroom. She issued a preliminary injunction against the owners on March 31, and on Sunday, April 2, the 232-day strike was finally over.

As I sat in the stuffy courtroom in Lower Manhattan that day it became so obvious how ill-prepared Major League Baseball's attorneys were to plead their case. During one moment, Judge Sotomayor reprimanded a baseball lawyer for lack of preparation.

So it came as no surprise when her decision was announced.

It took almost two more years for the two sides to finally reach agreement on a labor deal. That happened in November 1996.

Both sides learned from the dark days, the disastrous strike of 1994–95.

It's been called "the strike to end all strikes." There has never been a more accurate depiction.

Lessons learned have been enormous. The strike cut short what might have been baseball's greatest season in 50 years, but the game's recovery has been remarkable.

Owners and players have a much better relationship.

The 1994–95 strike was the eighth work stoppage in baseball history and, hopefully, its last.

The 2014 season will be the 19th with labor peace. Three contracts have been negotiated without a work stoppage or front-page rhetoric. When the current CBA expires in 2017, there will have been an unbelievable run of 22 years of labor peace. And during that period, there have been record-setting attendance and revenues, and a host of sweeping changes to the game.

Major league average salaries have risen from $1.88 million in 1994 to $3.65 million on Opening Day 2013. Industry revenues have increased 257 percent from $1.4 billion in 1994 to $7.5 billion in 2012.

Revenues are projected to reach $8.5 billion in 2014.

Selig says the greatest lesson learned has been "how tough it was bringing the sport back. It's taken a lot of blood, sweat, and tears. I hope the lesson learned by all parties is that we need to solve our problems quietly and sensibly. Our fans don't want to hear about this from either side."

With the 1994–95 strike over, Selig devised a 144-game schedule once the season resumed.

Fans were in a resentful and distrusting mood. The undertow was damaging.

But then the work ethic of Baltimore's Cal Ripken Jr. cleansed the atmosphere, and when on September 6, 1995, he surpassed Lou Gehrig's consecutive-game playing streak of 2,130 games, which had stood for 56 years, baseball's recovery was in full bloom.

No antidote could have been more effective.

I firmly believe that baseball stands alone with labor peace today because of lessons learned during the 1994–95 strike.

Selig deserves much of the credit.

He has been able to get MLB owners on the same page. That has been an enormous undertaking, an achievement that I believe has been the solid foundation for labor tranquilty.

If music is, in fact, the international language, baseball weaves a common thread throughout our society. It's where the CEO of a Fortune 500 company can freely—and comfortably—discuss the game on the same level with his storeroom clerk.

The late Ernie Harwell once wrote: "Baseball is a ballet without music. Drama without words. A carnival without kewpie dolls."

Yes, it is just a game, but it is America.

More than any other, it's a sport built on incredible performances, cherished memories and its treasured mementos. Every skill is measured, every number chronicled.

And yes, it's a sport that celebrates its triumphs and losses—deeds on the field and off the field—its incredible highs and excruciating lows.

5

A Family Game

O ctober 16th had come and gone.

It was now 12:16 the next morning as Aaron Boone stepped to the plate in the 11th inning at chilly Yankee Stadium in the seventh-and-deciding game of the 2003 American League Championship Series.

Red Sox 5, Yankees 5.

Boone crushed Tim Wakefield's first pitch, a knuckleball of course, and sent it trailing sparks to the left-field seats in the old, historic ballpark.

I was sitting in the second row of the press box and as the stadium and its 56,279 inhabitants went into a frenzy, I adjusted my earphones and listened to buddy Charley Steiner's call on WCBS Radio.

I knew this was historic and wanted to hear it:

"There's a fly ball, deep to left! It's on its way! There it goes! And the Yankees are going to the World Series! Aaron Boone has hit a home run! The Yankees go to the World Series for the 39th time in their remarkable history! Aaron Boone down the left-field line, they are waiting for him at home plate, and now he dives into the scrum! The Yankees win it 6–5!"

As impartial as sports journalists are expected to be, I must admit there were goose bumps that night.

My first thought was, *Somewhere, probably watching television, grandpa Ray Boone, a satisfied grin on this face, said to himself, 'Thatta way to go, boy. Thatta way to go! I'm so proud of you.'*

And I remembered back to those exciting afternoons at Philadelphia's Veterans Stadium in the late 1970s and 1980s when two little guys, not even 10 years old, batted and threw the ball with unbelievable talent for their ages as their dad, Bob Boone, prepared for his big-league game.

Aaron and older brother Bret hung out in the Phillies clubhouse with youngsters Pete Rose Jr., Ryan Luzinski, Mark McGraw, and Ruben Amaro Jr.

And, yes, grandpa Ray had to be proud.

Just like Gus Bell and Sam Hairston had to be when their grandsons followed in their footsteps to the major leagues.

Ditto Joe Coleman and Ducky Schofield.

In baseball's long and storied history there have been just five families that have produced three generations of major leaguers—the Boones (Ray, Bob, Bret, and Aaron); the Bells (Gus, Buddy, David, and Mike), the Hairstons (Sammy, Jerry, Johnny, Jerry Jr., and Scott), the Colemans (Joe, Joe Jr., and Casey), and the Schofield/Werths (Ducky Schofield, Dick Schofield, and Jayson Werth).

Werth is the grandson of Ducky Schofield and nephew of Dick Schofield, and also the stepson of Dennis Werth.

The Hairstons were the first African American family in this select group.

It should also be mentioned that the Runges—Ed, Paul, and Brian—make up a three-generation umpiring family.

There have been scores of sons who have followed in their fathers' footsteps.

In 1990, Ken Griffey Jr. and his father became the first son and father to play on the same team at the same time—for the Seattle Mariners.

In Griffey Sr.'s first game as a Mariner, on August 31, 1990, the pair hit back-to-back singles in the first inning and both scored.

On September 14, the pair hit back-to-back home runs in the top of the first off Angels pitcher Kirk McCaskill, becoming the first father-son duo to hit back-to-back homers.

The duo played a total of 51 games together before Griffey Sr. retired in June 1991.

It goes without saying, Griffey Jr. was one of his generation's best, and Griffey Sr. played nearly 20 years in the major leagues.

Griffey Jr., now 44, is a certain Hall of Famer—13 All-Star Games, 10 Gold Gloves, seven Silver Sluggers, 2,781 hits, 630 home runs, and 1,836 RBI. In 1997, the Kid won the AL MVP, hitting .304, smashing 56 homers, and driving in an amazing 147 runs. After his MVP campaign, he was voted to the MLB All-Century Team at the young age of 29.

In 2001, Tim Raines and Tim Raines Jr., also played as teammates with the Orioles.

Cecil and Prince Fielder is the only father-son combo to both hit 50 or more homers in a season. Papa Cecil blasted 51 in 1990. Seventeen years later, Prince hit 50.

From a historic standpoint, Jack Doscher, son of Herm Doscher, became the first second-generation MLB player when he made his debut with the Chicago Cubs in 1903.

But on August 19, 1992, Bret Boone, 23 at the time and playing for the Mariners, became the first-ever third-generation major leaguer in history.

At Baltimore's Camden Yards, second baseman Boone singled off Arthur Rhodes in the second inning and drove in a run in his first big-league at-bat. Boone was 1-for-4 in the Mariners' 10–8 victory.

On September 3, 1948, a 25-year-old infielder named Raymond Boone made his major league debut. A two-time All-Star, Boone batted .275 over 13 (1948–1960) big-league seasons. After that, he scouted 31 years for the Boston Red Sox.

His son, Bob Boone, now Washington Nationals assistant general manager and player development vice president, played 19 years (1972–1990) in the major leagues with the Phillies, Angels, and Royals. He later managed the Reds and Royals.

Bob was a career .254 hitter with 105 homers and 826 RBI in 2,264 games. He was an All-Star four times and as one of the top defensive catchers of his era, won seven Gold Gloves.

Only Ivan Rodriguez (13) and Johnny Bench (10) have won more Gold Gloves than Bob's seven. Boone caught 2,225 games, a record which was later broken by Carlton Fisk and Ivan Rodriguez.

Bret Boone is four years older than Aaron. A third brother, Matt, was drafted by the Detroit Tigers and after seven seasons in the minor leagues retired, having never made it to the majors.

Bret played in the major leagues 14 years (1992–2005) with five teams. A three-time All-Star, his best season was 2001 with the Seattle Mariners, when he batted .331, hit 37 homers, and led the American League with 141 runs batted in.

Aaron's career spanned 12 seasons (1997–2009) and during parts of three years (2001–2003), he played for his dad, Bob, who was the Cincinnati Reds manager. He had a lifetime batting average of .263, but will always be known for the homer he hit in the 2003 ALCS.

The Boones are descendants of American pioneer Daniel Boone.

David Russell "Gus" Bell, a four-time All-Star, played 15 years (1950–1964) in the major leagues, batting .281 with 206 homers and 942 RBI in 1,741 games. His best seasons were 1953 when he hit .300 with 30 homers and 105 RBI, and 1955 when he had a .308 average, 27 home runs, and 104 RBI. Four times he drove in 100 or more runs, and between 1953 and 1956 he slammed 103 home runs.

I vividly remember April 11, 1962. That was the day the Mets came to life, as dreadful as they were. Bell, like so many premier players near the end of their careers, was the Mets' starting right fielder in their first game. He was their first baserunner after hitting a single in the second inning. St. Louis won 11–4.

David Gus "Buddy" Bell played his first major league game on April 15, 1972, for the Cleveland Indians. He played 18 years (1972–1989) for four teams, compiling a lifetime .279 mark.

Buddy was a five-time All-Star, won six Gold Gloves, one Silver Slugger Award, and the 1988 Lou Gehrig Memorial Award.

Now a Chicago White Sox vice president and assistant general manager, Bell is a former manager of the Tigers, Rockies, and Royals.

David Bell played 12 years (1995–2006) for six teams. On April 15, 1998, he hit the first inside-the-park home run at Cleveland's Jacobs Field. He made major league history on June 28, 2004, when he joined his late grandfather, becoming the first grandfather-grandson duo to hit for the cycle.

David achieved his cycle in 2004 for the Phillies against the Montreal Expos; Grandpa Bell hit his on June 4, 1951, in the Pittsburgh Pirates' 12–4 win against the Phillies. He's currently assistant hitting coach for the St. Louis Cardinals.

Michael John Bell was selected by Texas in the first round of the 1993 draft. He played his first big-league game for the hometown Cincinnati Reds on July 20, 2000, and ended his one-season career on October 1, even though he played in the minor leagues several more seasons, with coaching and managerial stints. He's now director of player development for the Diamondbacks.

A third Bell son, Ricky, was drafted by the Dodgers in the third round in 1997 and played in the minor leagues for 10 seasons.

Jerry Hairston Jr. retired in 2013, six decades after his grandfather Sammy Hairston played and almost 40 years after his father, Jerry, debuted with the Chicago White Sox in 1973.

Sam Hairston, who died in 1997 at age 77, had only the briefest stint in the major leagues—four games, two hits (one a double), and an RBI in five at-bats (two walks) for the 1951 White Sox.

Jerry Hairston Sr. played 14 seasons (1973–1989) and except for 51 games with Pittsburgh in 1977 followed by three years (1978–1980) with Durango of the Mexican League, spent his entire career with the Chicago White Sox. His lifetime batting average was .258. He specialized as a pinch hitter.

On April 15, 1983, Hairston broke up a perfect game by the Tigers' Milt Wilcox when he singled with two out in the ninth inning. His brother, Johnny Hairston, played three games for the Chicago Cubs in 1969.

Jerry Jr. had been in the major leagues since 1998, when he broke in with the Baltimore Orioles. The 2013 season, his second with the Los Angeles Dodgers as a utility man, was his 16th and final. He joined their broadcast team for the 2014 season.

Scott Hairston, younger brother of Jerry Jr., made his major league debut with Arizona in 2004. He spent the 2013 season with the Cubs and Nationals.

The Coleman clan is the first third-generation family to achieve the distinction on the mound. All three were right-handers.

Joseph Patrick Coleman pitched 10 seasons (1942, 1946–1955) in the major leagues, eight of which were with the Philadelphia Athletics. His best season was 1948, when he was 14–13 and pitched in the All-Star Game.

At Sportsman's Park in St. Louis, Coleman shut out the National League All-Stars and held them hitless over the last three innings, to save a 5–2 victory for Vic Raschi and the AL.

His son, Joseph Howard Coleman, pitched 15 years (1965–1979) in the major leagues after making his debut on September 28, 1965, at the age of 18. He was 2–0 that month, with two complete games and a 1.50 earned run average.

He was one of the most highly touted young players in 1965, when he was selected third overall by the Senators in the first-ever amateur draft. Coleman reached a quick agreement with the Senators, and after a summer in the minors was called up in late September.

During his tenure with the Senators, he often clashed with his manager, Ted Williams.

The Hall of Famer insisted that Coleman throw sliders. Coleman believed the pitch would hurt his arm.

"No matter how hard I tried," Coleman told Ed Rumill of the *Christian Science Monitor*, "I couldn't change Ted's mind. He didn't like my stubborn attitude and didn't yield an inch."

Williams eventually pulled Coleman from the rotation and banished him to the bullpen. Coleman's best season was 1973 with the Tigers, when he was 23–15 with a 3.53 earned run average.

The year before he was 19–14 with a 2.80 ERA and nine complete games. He was selected for the All-Star Game at Atlanta Stadium, but did not pitch.

Coleman's solid season helped the Tigers to the American League Championship Series against Oakland. Coleman kept the A's from sweeping the best-of-five series when he pitched a 3–0, complete-game shutout, striking out 14. The A's won the series in five games.

His son, Casey, pitched his first game in the big leagues on August 2, 2010. He was with the Cubs in 2011 and '12, but pitched the 2013 season with Iowa of the Pacific Coast League.

Sam Hairston was much more successful in the Negro Leagues.

"I know my grandfather loved playing baseball," said Hairston Jr. "I remembered the stories he used to tell us. Because of those stories, that's why I wanted to play. I wanted to have stories of my own.

"Because of him, I knew about Josh Gibson, Jackie Robinson, Satchel Paige, Cool Papa Bell, and Double Duty Radcliffe before it became cool."

Sam was the White Sox's first American-born African American player; Cuban-born Minnie Minoso was their first black player, three months earlier.

Hairston Jr., in a 2009 interview with the *Cincinnati Enquirer's* John Erardi, said, "My father [Jerry Sr.] is proud of being the bridge for three generations in baseball."

When Jerry Jr.'s younger brother, Scott, broke in with the Diamondbacks in May 2004, he became the fifth of the Hairston clan to make it to the majors—a record for three-generation families.

Former White Sox general manager Roland Hemond recalled in 2010, "Sam Hairston told me when Jerry Jr. and Scott were probably 10 and 8 that they would become major league players. He was right."

"Scott can really mash that high fastball like Dad could," Hairston Sr. says. "Not many guys can do that. When you watch Scott hit, you're watching my father—like a carbon copy."

Sam was a favorite in the Negro Leagues. In a published story, he once blasted a home run over a light tower in Nashville when word came over the public-address system that his wife had just given birth to a son, Johnny, back in Birmingham. In the 1948 Negro League East-West All-Star Game, played in Chicago, he was 7-for-8. He played until he was 40, then scouted and coached until he died.

"I cannot tell you how many times I've had coaches and players from other organizations come up to me and say what kind of influence my grandfather had on them," Hairston Jr. told Erardi.

"I think of my grandfather all the time. Maybe that's why I'm so intense. I don't want to waste it. Sometimes I get a little too emotional, because I care so much. My father's talked to me about that. He says, 'Don't try to carry the burden so much; your grandfather would be proud of you no matter what you do.'

"But, it's who we are. We care about playing well. We care about helping our team win. My grandfather used to dwell on that. I feel like I'm playing for him—for the chance he never really got."

Said Jerry Sr.: "My dad never got a chance to see Jerry and Scott play. He died the year Jerry signed. We drove to Birmingham in May that year. He hit Jerry some ground balls, and Jerry took some batting practice. My father said this kid's going to be a major leaguer."

When Sam Hairston would relate baseball stories to his son, Jerry says "that inspired me to want to experience baseball. It just seemed to be the thing to do. That's something my dad helped me appreciate and I passed it onto my kids. The first and most important thing is the desire to play."

Coincidentally, Bret Boone was working as a TV analyst for the 2003 ALCS.

"Hey, you stink right now," Bret remembers telling his brother, who had struggled for two months, was hitless in Game 6, and relegated to the bench for the series against Boston. "But do something tomorrow and everyone will forget all about that."

Joe Torre, Yankees manager at the time, remembers, "Aaron is a great competitor, but he was just jumping at the ball all that series. He was trying to hit the ball right out of the pitcher's hand. I got up and went over to him and said, 'Just try to hit a single to right. It doesn't mean you won't hit a home run to left.'"

"Now, in the last couple of years, I appreciate the moment a lot more," says Aaron Boone, now an ESPN analyst. "I feel thankful that I got to be in that situation, on that stage, to have a small part in such a huge rivalry. So many people I come across have a personal story attached to that moment. I've learned to embrace the fact that a lot of people know me for that."

The glow from Aaron Boone's dramatic home run was short-lived.

During the off-season, he tore a knee ligament playing in a pick-up basketball game—a violation of his contract with the Yankees.

As a matter of trivia, had Aaron not suffered the serious injury, Alex Rodriguez might never have become a Yankee.

On February 26, 2004, the Yanks cut Boone from their roster. He was replaced at third base by A-Rod, who was obtained from the Texas Rangers. It's doubtful the Yankees would have tried to obtain Rodriguez in the blockbuster deal had Boone not suffered the injury.

The Yankees made overtures of re-signing Aaron Boone later in 2004 to play second base in 2005 when he was fully recovered, but instead he signed a two-year deal with the Indians.

When asked how proud he is of his sons, Bob Boone says, "I'm most proud of the fact that my kids turned out to be tremendous citizens and they happened to fall into something that they could excel in. The avenue just happened to be baseball.

"For whatever reason, our family was picked out and blessed with that talent. We're proud of it and I know the Bells are very proud of it as a family. To have your kids go into an occupation they love and it happens to be daddy's occupation, there's probably some ego involved in that. But if Bret or Aaron had gone into something else, I'd be just as proud of them."

On the last day of the 1998 season, the Reds helped Bret Boone make baseball trivia history by starting the only infield ever composed of two sets of brothers: first baseman Stephen Larkin, second baseman Bret Boone, future Hall of Fame shortstop Barry Larkin, and third baseman Aaron Boone.

During a 1991 interview, Ray Boone said: "Bret came out of the womb hitting. He lived with us when Bob was doing his six months military service. Bret was barely two years old, but every day I'd be out there in the backyard throwing Wiffle balls to him. Bret crushed so many balls over the house that I called [former manager] Dave Garcia and told him to come watch the kid. Dave took one look at his swing and offered to sign him."

Athletics are a huge part of the Boone pedigree.

Patricia Boone, Ray's wife and Bob's mother, and her twin sister, Martha, were synchronized swimmers and appeared in several Esther Williams movies.

Martha, who's 87, was a teaching golf pro and just recently Bob says, "gave me a lesson."

Patricia Boone died in 2008. During an interview I did with her in 1993 for *USA TODAY*, she said she never regretted the hundreds of hours behind the wheel of the family station wagon driving her children to Spring Training from California when Ray was playing.

"It was drive there, then back home again for school, then when school was out whatever city Ray was playing in."

She added, "At the youngest age, Bob was always on the field with Ray. That gave him a tremendous advantage. Same thing with Bret and Aaron with their dad.

"So many mothers ask me how I could do it—driving them around and all that. I think because they were in sports they were great kids. For me, seeing their accomplishments made it all worthwhile."

Bret says when his dad was with the Phillies, "I wanted to go to the ballpark every day. If Dad wouldn't let me, my day was ruined. I just loved it. It was nothing but a positive thing for me. We used to have myself, my brother Aaron, Greg Luzinski's son, Pete Rose's son, Tug McGraw's kids, Steve Carlton's kids. There were quite a few of us hanging around, probably driving the players crazy."

Bret remembers that Tug McGraw taught him how to make behind-the-back catches.

"My dad was an influence. He worked with me all the time, mostly on pitching," Bob told me, referring to Ray. "He let me play and instilled in me the fact the game has to be fun and that's the way you play it. Watching the kind of player my dad was and being around ballparks my entire life certainly helped.

"I wanted to be a ballplayer from the first time I can remember. I got great instruction from the time I could walk. My kids were raised the exact same way."

Those memories of Bret and Aaron shagging fly balls at Veterans Stadium keep coming back.

"If I left for the park before they got home from school they were very upset with me," says Bob. "It's changed now, but I'm so thankful to the Phillies that they allowed the kids to be there. That's the only time you can see and help raise your kids, at least for half of the year, and have any kind of influence on them. That was a great time and a great time for those kids growing up."

There is an obvious intimidation factor about playing in the major leagues, but I'm convinced youngsters who hang around ballparks with their big-league-playing dads have an advantage. They take it for granted.

Bob wholeheartedly agrees.

"They got to learn and be around stars and superstars," he says. "The biggest thing from all that is the major leagues wasn't intimidating. When they finally got the opportunity to go to a big-league environment it was like, 'I know Steve Carlton and Pete Rose and Greg Luzinski.' That's a big hurdle for a lot of the players."

How proud?

"I was extremely proud when Bret became the first, knowing the odds are against any of us to get there," he says. "My dad's influence and my influence was, 'Hey, you can do whatever you want. I'm not pushing anyone to baseball.'"

Yet Bob adds all the kids growing up felt that pressure: "Hey, I'm Ray Boone's son; I'm Bob Boone's son. We were all aware of that, but also aware of when you get on the baseball field it doesn't matter whose son you."

Regardless, for anyone with an enduring passion for baseball, growing up in a major league family is unique—a dream most of us can hardly fathom.

Bob remembers his father, elected the AL's starting third baseman and representing Detroit, hit a home run for the American League in their 11–9 victory in the 1954 All-Star Game.

"That was special," he says.

Bob Boone, born November 19, 1947, says "I was at the 1948 World Series with my father. It was his first year in the majors. I was nine months old; I don't remember, but I was there."

Ray Boone was with Cleveland; the Indians played the Boston Braves and won the Series.

Bob does recall that during his dad's final three years he was with four teams. "When he was traded to the White Sox in 1958, I got to go to the ballpark every day. I was so big they let me wear Nellie Fox's uniform. I got to shag fly balls during batting practice with the sons of Early Wynn and Earl Torgeson."

And there was this, maybe Ray Boone's most fulfilling dream, if not thrill:

Ray, Bob (then the Cincinnati Reds manager), and the family were at the 2003 All-Star Game at Chicago's U.S. Cellular Field and watched Bret and Aaron both play in the game, won by the American League 7–6.

"Dad was getting older then, but he was so thrilled," says Bob. "We have a picture of the two boys, me, and him."

Ray Boone died the following year, on October 17 at age 81.

Throughout our conversation, Bob didn't seem to put the third-generation topic down, but kept trying to put it in perspective.

"We're all very proud of it, but we all had our own careers," he says. "We understood that it was special, but we didn't live that it was special. It was their profession, our profession. I'd help the boys and throw batting practice as my dad did with me."

Pausing, he muses: "The three-generation thing really transcends baseball. I'm very proud of my kids, and proud of my dad.

"But it really wasn't about baseball. It was about who they were and what they became.

"From our standpoint, the Boones were first and the only ones that had three who played in the All-Star Game. It's neat, but in the total scheme of things it's really about the people they are."

Buddy Bell agrees with Bob about the advantage youngsters of major leaguers have making it to the big time.

"He's 100 percent right," said Buddy. "I respected the players, but my dad always made sure I respected the people off the field— the cops, the trainers, the writers, ushers. Quite frankly, some of my best friends come from that group.

"I was never really intimidated by the clubhouse or the players."

He believes there will be more and more third-generation families.

"The money is so much better today," he told me. "My dad never really pushed me because he wanted me to make a career out of something else—a career that had more longevity. The money back then wasn't great. Today, because of the money, youngsters are pushed more.

"This may sound funny, but I kind of thought everybody's father played ball. I put my dad on a pedestal because he was my father, not because he played ball."

When Buddy was growing up in Cincinnati, he says he didn't spend much time at the ballpark because players' children weren't allowed.

"In those days management respected the players' space in the clubhouse. On the other hand, my kids were always around— shagging in the outfield during batting practice and all that."

Buddy said most of his fond memories growing up were about being with his dad's teammates—"Joe Nuxhall, Wally Post, Ted Kluszewski, Frank Robinson, Vada Pinson, and Billy Martin. More than anything those personalities, the fun they were having piqued my interest."

In a 1985 interview with the *Cincinnati Enquirer*, Gus Bell said Buddy "used to come with me quite a bit. If I was injured or anything and had to work hard, he'd always come out. Shag fly balls and stuff like that. He always wanted to play ball. If Buddy hadn't played professional ball, he's one of those guys who'd have looked for a Sunday league and played until he was 50 years old."

And finally, away from the major leagues, there is the story of the Acerras, an all-brother baseball team that barnstormed in the Northeast during the 1940s and '50s.

The team consisted of 12 brothers, and in 1997 the National Baseball Hall of Fame recognized the Acerras and identified as many as 15 all-brother teams, from the Skillicorns to the Gillums to the Coombses and the Van Tassels.

According to Audrey Vernick's 2012 book *Brothers at Bat: The True Story of an Amazing All-Brother Baseball Team,* the Acerra family had 16 children, including 12 baseball-playing boys. It was the 1930s, and many families had lots of kids. But only one had enough to field a baseball team—with three on the bench! The Acerras were the longest-playing all-brother team in baseball history. They loved the game, but more important, they cared for and supported each other and stayed together as a team.

Is a fourth generation possible?

Bob Boone has a grandson, Bret's oldest child, Jacob, a freshman in high school.

"Talk about pressure," Bob Boone says, with a chuckle. "Man, you got some heat on you. You've got a lot of water to tote here. He's a pretty good player and we'll have to see what happens."

6

Baseball Chatter

Years ago, Skip Sailer, a stockbroker friend, jumped up from behind his desk and shouted, "I just hit a home run—with the bases loaded!"

I didn't see the ball leave his office, or runners circling the desk. But, for sure, it was a *home run*.

What Sailer was celebrating was a stock deal that was paying huge dividends—a home run!

Few people can go a full day without using a baseball term in their conversations. Baseball is truly our national pastime, but it's also an integral part of our vocabulary. Baseball terminology is steeped in tradition; it's light and fits well in our society. The language of baseball transcends eras. No other sport has introduced so many words, so many phrases that are used daily by just about everyone.

That the influence of baseball on American English at large is stunning and strong is brilliantly described in *The Old Ball Game* by Tristram Potter Coffin.

He wrote: "No other sport and few other occupations have introduced so many phrases, so many words, so many twists into our language as has baseball. The true test comes in the fact that old ladies who have never been to a ballpark, coquettes who don't know or care who's on first, men who think athletics begin and end with a pair of goal posts, still know and use a great deal of baseball-derived terminology. Perhaps other sports in their efforts to replace baseball as 'our national pastime' have two strikes on them before they come to bat."

Yes, when an outcome or an event goes the wrong way "I struck out."

An important member of a negotiating team will "bat clean-up."

A person solving most of the issues of a problem will "circle the bases."

When I make a strong remark without hesitation, it's "a fastball down the middle."

When a person is not totally honest or upfront, "he threw me a curveball."

An extremely long, exhausting meeting lasted into "extra innings."

A guy on his first date: "I couldn't get to first base!"

When a speaker was unable to make it to the convention "a pinch-hitter was summoned."

In a tough negotiation: "They're playing hardball with us."

Or when someone is forced to do something: "It was a squeeze play."

Talking about someone's performance: Her "batting average" is pretty high.

Or if someone makes a glaring mistake, it was "a bonehead play."

During a tremendously successful endeavor or performance: "He's batting a thousand."

When someone is near failure: "She has two strikes against her."

Or times when a person isn't focused or paying attention he's told, "keep your eye on the ball."

When a situation completely changes: "It's a whole new ballgame."

When a person takes quick action and leaves, it was a "hit and run."

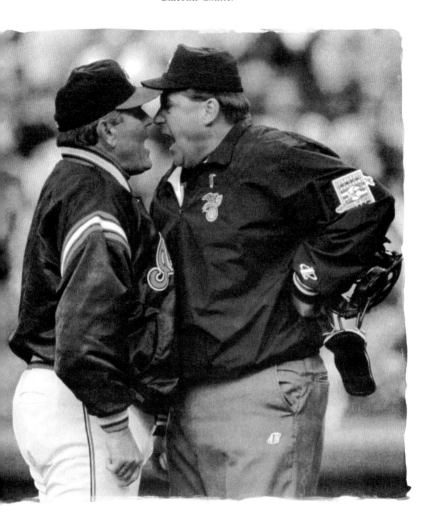

A quick action, with no hesitation, might be "right off the bat."
A person successful in difficult situations is "a clutch hitter."
The first speaker or presenter at a function is "leading off."
Often the next person up is "on deck."
A complete analysis by someone can be defined as "he touched
all the bases."

Or someone not tuned in to the subject or issue "is out in left field."

When someone is supportive, it could be said he "went to bat" for you.

A long detailed discussion is often a "play-by-play" of the subject.

During negotiations when agreement is close: "You're in the ballpark."

Not quite measuring up is frequently termed "minor league."

An unacceptable or unkind gesture is "bush league."

When a negotiation or event is near the end it's "in the ninth inning."

Working with someone, or agreeing, you're "playing ball" with them.

Or, when someone disagrees, they're "refusing to play ball."

When someone voices a strong opinion or tries to convince others, it's "a grandstand play" or he's a "grandstander."

A man or woman looking for a date can often be described as "playing the field."

Someone called in to help may have been summoned "from the bullpen."

From Paul Dickson's definitive work *The Dickson Baseball Dictionary,* he turned to Elting E Morison, who described baseball language in *American Heritage* this way:

"Why is baseball terminology so dominant an influence in the language? Does it suggest that the situations that develop as the game is played are comparable to the patterns of our daily work? Does the sport imitate the fundamentals of the national life or is the national life shaped to an extent by the character of the sport?"

He answers his question by quoting Hall of Famer Reggie Jackson.

"The country is as American as baseball."

7

George Steinbrenner's American Dream

He was born on the Fourth of July.

He was big on stars and stripes, but even more about pinstripes.

He frequently set off fireworks, but not just on his birthday.

He was a visionary and a bully. He was quick-tempered, combative, a soft-touch for charities and those in need and, at times loveable, and a very good man—all in one.

It's impossible to tell about baseball in America without discussing the Boss, the late George M. Steinbrenner III, and the New York Yankees.

For decades they went hand in hand.

Until Steinbrenner died—and could this have been more coincidental?—the day of the All-Star Game in Anaheim, California, on July 13, 2010, he was the face of the Yankees, if not all Major League Baseball.

There is no sports franchise in the world more renowned, more recognizable, more loved and hated, than the New York Yankees.

Players insist there's a special feeling when they pull on the renowned Yankee pinstripes. They're as much a part of this team as the universally worn interlocking NY.

And the former shipbuilder from Cleveland greatly enriched this enduring legacy.

Once, during a long give-and-take session in his Tampa office, the subject of the struggling Montreal Expos came up. It was mentioned the Yankees paid $34 million in luxury tax and another $75.9 million in revenue sharing that year, both practices designed with the intent of making the rich franchises help to keep the struggling, small-market teams solvent.

"Look, I didn't buy the Montreal Expos," he almost shouted, slapping a hand on his desk. "I bought the New York Yankees. It's crazy when you cannot make money. I'd like to see everybody competing, but we're not a socialist state."

Yes, he bought the New York Yankees, and until his failing health kept him away, life was never the same in the Bronx.

Steinbrenner put together a group who purchased the then-faltering franchise from CBS for $8.7 million on January 3, 1973.

According to *Forbes* magazine the Yankees are now worth $2.3 billion, surpassing the Dallas Cowboys' $2.1 billion as the most valuable franchise in North America.

I remember attending a press conference in New York when the sale was announced, with the obviously energetic Steinbrenner telling reporters he wouldn't be a hands-on owner.

"We plan absentee ownership as far as running the Yankees is concerned," he said. "We're not going to pretend we're something we aren't. I'll stick to building ships."

Nothing could have been further from the truth.

He pumped money and energy into the mostly dormant franchise. Before long, he was dominating the back pages of the New York tabloids, a practice he sought and thrived on.

Quickly nicknamed "the Boss," he soon became baseball's biggest spender, wheeling and dealing, spending millions in the free-agent market to stock the Yankees.

To say George Steinbrenner became big in New York is an understatement.

"When you're a shipbuilder, nobody pays any attention to you," he said. "But when you own the New York Yankees…they do, and I love it."

And then added: "Owning the Yankees is like owning the *Mona Lisa*."

During the 25 years (1982–2007) I was baseball editor for *USA TODAY* Steinbrenner and I had a solid, sometimes bumpy, yet warm working relationship.

He was always accessible and frequently initiated the call, usually to blast me over a story or, as was his behind-the-scenes method, plant an item that would obviously get to the player or incident he had on his mind. He always talked about how much he loved his players, but that didn't stop him from insulting them if the notion struck.

We had a large property in Delaware with nearly two acres of grass. When I was younger, I'd often spend hours mowing the lawn.

Late one afternoon, Steinbrenner urgently called and was told by my wife, Patricia, that, "Hal's out on the tractor cutting the grass."

"Go get him," Pat says he bellowed over the phone. "Tell him it's the Boss and I want to talk to him."

Whatever the reason for the call, he never let me forget about the grass.

He'd often verbally put me down, ordering, "You better go cut the grass. I'm told it's pretty tall."

Or at Yankee Stadium for a game: "Why are you here? You should be home cutting that grass!"

The Yankees became the richest of franchises and spending money never stopped the Boss.

He said it was easier and faster to "buy" a team rather than build one from the grass roots of the minor leagues.

In 1977, the Yankees won their first World Series since 1962, when they defeated the Dodgers in six games.

It was Steinbrenner's first World Series title and it came after he had landed Reggie Jackson and Catfish Hunter, baseball's most expensive free agents at the time.

The Yankees repeated, winning another title over the Dodgers in 1978.

The Yanks also appeared in the 1981 World Series against the Dodgers, but lost. That prompted Steinbrenner, front and center, to issue a public apology to New York and Yankees fans for the disappointing seven-game setback.

Money was no object.

Despite the turmoil he created and his bombastic personality, the Yankees thrived.

Under Steinbrenner, the Yankees won 11 American League pennants and seven World Series.

His last was in 2009. His health was deteriorating and he was seldom in New York from his Tampa home. The Yankees defeated the Phillies in six games under manager Joe Girardi.

Following their baptism as the New York Yankees in 1903 after being transplanted as the Baltimore Orioles, they've won 27 World Series, 40 pennants, and been in 51 postseasons.

No franchise has had the steady stream of legends—Babe Ruth, Lou Gehrig, Joe DiMaggio, Phil Rizzuto, Yogi Berra, Roger Maris, Mickey Mantle, Whitey Ford, Bobby Murcer, Lou Piniella, Reggie Jackson, Elston Howard, Don Mattingly, Derek Jeter, Mariano Rivera, and many, many others.

Managers from John McGraw to Joe McCarthy to Casey Stengel to Joe Torre to Girardi are all woven into the history of this great franchise—all so much an integral part of the fabric of baseball in America.

This should tell you something about the legendary Yankees: Sixteen numbers—most of any team—have been retired, including Jackie Robinson's 42. Rivera's, which is also 42, joined the list in 2013.

The Yankees, more than any other team, have etched unforgettable moments in baseball's rich history.

How many times have you seen clips of dying Lou Gehrig's farewell "luckiest man on the face of the earth" speech on July 4, 1939, or Babe Ruth's farewell wave of the cap to the crowd in his last game?

Gehrig teamed with Babe Ruth to form baseball's most devastating hitting tandem ever. The Iron Horse had 13 consecutive

seasons with both 100 runs scored and 100 RBI, averaging 139 runs and 147 RBI; set an American League mark with 184 RBI in 1931; hit a record 23 grand slams; and won the 1934 Triple Crown. His .361 batting average in seven World Series led the Yankees to six titles.

Gehrig's consecutive games-played streak ended at 2,130, when he was felled by a disease that later carried his name. The streak was later broken by Baltimore's Cal Ripken Jr. in 1995.

Gehrig's No. 4 was the first number ever retired in Major League Baseball.

So many moments. Reggie Jackson hitting three consecutive home runs in the 1977 World Series. The 1961 home run duel between Roger Maris and Mickey Mantle. And Maris, of course, breaking Babe Ruth's 1927 home run record of 60 in '61.

Or the references to the 1927 Yankees' "Murderers' Row."

Take nothing away from that history, but for me talk about the Yankees always comes full circle to Steinbrenner.

Once I wrote he issued more pink slips than Victoria's Secret.

During his reign, often called a "reign of terror," he went through 15 managers. He fired Billy Martin five times, but kept bringing him back.

In the Boss' first 23 seasons, he switched managers 20 times, including the hiring and firing of Martin, and went through 11 general managers in 30 seasons.

The least little misstep could cost a front-office employee his or her job. On one occasion he fired a media director because he refused to come to work on a holiday.

Despite the pink slips, Steinbrenner remained loyal. Most times when managers or GMs were fired, he kept them on in another capacity.

"George is a great guy, unless you have to work for him," said Lou Piniella, who managed the Yankees twice in the 1980s.

The Boss often fought with other owners, commissioners and umpires.

One time during a playoff game, he virtually pulled me from my press-box seat, marched me to the video room, and ordered me to watch a video replay of a blown call by an umpire.

"That's what we have to put up with," he bellowed. "Write it!"

He was twice suspended from the game—the first time by Commissioner Bowie Kuhn in 1974 for pleading guilty to the felony crime of making illegal contributions to Richard Nixon's presidential campaign.

In 1990, Commissioner Fay Vincent handed down a lifetime suspension for paying a gambler named Howie Spira $40,000 to dig up dirt on Yankees player Dave Winfield, whom Steinbrenner labeled "Mr. May" because of his lack of production later in the season.

The ban was lifted in 1993.

Vincent, an obvious adversary, said this about Steinbrenner in the *New York Times*: "He was intensely belligerent. He never waited to attack from the flank. Nor was he subtle. He took things on directly and seldom ducked a punch. And that style worked for him.

"But he cared about our great game and could be counted on for support when I needed it."

When MLB fined Steinbrenner for criticizing umpires in a playoff series with the Seattle Mariners, he had accumulated disciplinary fines totaling $645,000.

That never bothered him because he was so impatient, so driven that there was no way he could sit back when something went against his grain.

One time I was invited into his New York hotel suite at the Regency. When I walked in, I was greeted by a full-sized cutout of John Wayne. And then, before I sat down, he presented me with a book on Gen. George Patton.

"Read this," he said. "It tells a lot about how we should approach baseball."

Steinbrenner idolized Patton and Gen. Douglas MacArthur and I believe he pictured himself as a general, not the Yankees owner.

Before he became involved in professional sports, Steinbrenner was a multisport athlete at Culver Military Academy and later an assistant football coach at Northwestern and Purdue.

Said Derek Jeter about Steinbrenner's demanding, impatient approach to winning: "The thing with the Boss, he's an old football coach. So his way was he sort of looked at the baseball season like we played 12 games and we had to win every single day."

Steinbrenner, typical of anyone born on July 4th, envisioned himself a patriot and ordered "God Bless America" be played at Yankee Stadium during the seventh-inning stretch. Other teams dropped the practice soon after it was adopted following the 9/11 terrorist attacks on the World Trade Center.

When he hired Joe Torre on the recommendation of the late Arthur Richman, he landed the most successful skipper of the Steinbrenner era.

Steinbrenner is the first to tell you he and Torre had their differences.

"Joe and I understand each other," he once told me. "He's one of the best managers I've ever had, and I've had some good ones. He's a great one."

After nine years on the job, Torre's wife, Ali, told me: "I think Joe's much more at peace with George now than he was last spring [2004]. "He's settled in and [with a contract extension] knows what he's going to be dong the next three seasons."

Beginning in 1996, Torre took the Yankees to the postseason each of his 12 years. He won the World Series four of his first five years, missing out in 1997. Overall, his teams went to the Fall Classic six times.

Since 1995, the Yankees have failed to play in the postseason just two times—2008 and 2013.

Nothing, however, was more devastating to Steinbrenner and the Yankees than 2004 against the rival Boston Red Sox.

After taking a three games to none lead in the best-of-seven American League Championship Series, the Yankees needed just three outs in the ninth inning of Game 4 to return to the World Series.

The Red Sox, however, rallied to tie 4–4 and went on to win the game 6–4 on David Ortiz's two-run, 12th-inning home run. The Red Sox won the next three games and then swept the St. Louis Cardinals to win the World Series for the first time since 1918.

That was the World Series which enabled them to exorcise "the Curse of the Bambino," inflicted on the Red Sox after Babe Ruth was sold to the Yankees in 1919.

I sat in his memorabilia-cluttered office above Legends Field (it's since been re-named George M. Steinbrenner Field) during Spring Training in 2005 and asked about the devastating loss to Boston.

"It hurts," he said with a painful look in his eyes. "They were a good team, and they beat us. That's all, they beat us. I hate to lose any way, you know, but to lose the way we lost is tough. That was one of the toughest things I've been through in my life.

"Yeah, it really hurt. But I just came back here to Tampa and started planning on what we have to do to get back to the World Series. I just hope we get there." (They didn't.)

A year later, I once again visited with him. It was obvious to me his health was failing. His speech was slower and he chose his words much more carefully.

We made small talk—about his horses, baseball, and the upcoming World Baseball Classic, which he deplored. It was one of the last extended interviews he gave. I chuckled and said, "Boss, have you really mellowed?"

"Not mellow-mellow," he said, sitting back in his chair and adjusting a button on his blue denim shirt with the familiar NY emblem on the pocket.

I asked how long he planned to run the Yankees and there was hesitation. "The kids, the boys Hank and Hal, are coming in, doing more and more. You have to let the young elephants into the tent."

This man, known to inflict terror on anyone who in his opinion didn't measure up, had been almost a recluse the past 18 months. He gave few interviews, instead issuing statements on key issues.

"I was in the press too much," he said. "So many times they'd write not what I said, but something else. I just got tired of that, having to explain myself. So now I'd rather think about what I'm going to say and write it down."

Without asking, he volunteered: "Mellowed? I haven't mellowed, not in my desire to win. No, I haven't mellowed in a lot of ways, but I'm not quite the way I used to be. But I'm still very demanding."

I asked his good friend Donald Trump his thoughts and in typical fashion the Donald said, "George will never mellow, and I don't want him to. There's nobody like him and I don't want him to change."

The new billion-dollar-plus Yankee Stadium is a much tamer place with son Hal running the team. Even though the Yankees' payroll remains the highest in the major leagues, the young Steinbrenner is attempting to show financial restraint.

From 1973 until he died—a span of over 37 years, Steinbrenner's Yankees created a success no other team could equal.

There were the seven World Series titles, the 11 pennants, and the winning percentage of .566.

Those are just the numbers.

It's really the aura of George M. Steinbrenner that continues.

8

Cox, La Russa, Torre —End of an Era

One by one their names were called—Bobby Cox, Joe Torre, Tony La Russa.

And then they buttoned their spanking new shirts with "Hall of Fame" scripted across the front and it was a glorious celebration for baseball. Together, they own 7,558 wins, eight World Series championships, and almost a century—actually 91 years—of living the uncertain life of a major league manager.

When this legendary troika was unanimously elected to the Hall of Fame in December 2013 it signaled the end of an era.

They were the faces of their teams—each just as much a celebrity as the players who controlled their destiny. They had rock-star status.

Consider this: During 1996, Torre's first year, the Yankees finished seventh among the 14 American League teams in attendance at 2.2 million. By 2007, they were first, drawing 4.2 million, and he was a huge reason why.

Only Connie Mack (3,731) and John McGraw (2,763) won more games than La Russa (2,728), Cox (2,504), and Torre (2,326), and that comes from a list of the 680 who've managed in the 137 years Major League Baseball has been around.

Only 23 managers have been invited to join this special Hall of Fame fraternity. I predict getting there in the future will be much more difficult.

Oh, the door isn't being slammed shut; it's just that baseball managing is dramatically changing. Producing the credentials Cox, Torre, and La Russa possessed will be almost impossible even for the brightest young skippers.

In years to come Jim Leyland, Lou Piniella, Bruce Bochy, and Davey Johnson could find their way to Cooperstown. No question, they're deserving, but their splendid careers fall a few steps behind the newest Hall of Famers.

It's more than a changing of the guard. None of the above reached the magical 2,000-win plateau.

Earl Weaver, Whitey Herzog, Sparky Anderson, Tommy Lasorda, and Dick Williams were a generation behind Cox, Torre, and La Russa. They were from the same mold.

These all were managers who defined the role we've come to know.

Today, it's a different game. The job has changed. It's unlikely any of the new breed will be able to sustain the types of careers their predecessors have built.

Most managers today are an extension of their general manager, the executive wing. They're tied to computer-generated analytical studies of players and teams. They alone seldom make all the on-field decisions.

Seat-of-the-pants managing is now as outdated as complete-game pitchers.

When La Russa was earning his stripes with Oakland in the mid-1980s, I often identified him as a "state-of-the-art" manager. He was a fierce competitor, but more innovative than anyone in the business. He had tremendous impact on the game.

He pioneered the use of the specialized bullpen and the one-inning closer. He tried using a left-handed third baseman with the White Sox in 1983 and 1984. He and his pitching guru, Dave Duncan, experimented with a three-man rotation.

I was sitting with Tony one night in Spring Training and he kept looking off into space. "I'm thinking about tomorrow's [exhibition] game," he finally told me. "I have some things I want to try."

And yet when his election to the Hall of Fame was announced, he shrugged off his innovations.

"I've never invented anything, but always somebody taught me something," he said.

In this new era, I compare Tampa Bay's Joe Maddon to La Russa, although it's doubtful Tony subscribes to the new genre.

Joe is my modern-day state-of-the-art manager. With a ridiculously low payroll, he's guided the Rays to the postseasons four of the last six years. They've won 90 or more games the last four years.

He agrees the election of Cox, Torre, and La Russa is the end of an era for managers.

"I think Jimmy Leyland should go, but the omnipotent manager is no longer going to exist," he said. "In the past, organizations rotated around managers. In the next several years teams are going to revolve around managers and general managers, and front offices.

"There's got to be more of a marriage between both to co-exist in today's world. We do it that way in Tampa Bay. I think that's the right way to do it.

"The way the game has evolved, looking for edges, and really trying to make better decisions based on high finance, you don't want to rely on the older techniques.

"Moving forward, the young manager who's willing to work with the front office and create this marriage with that section or sector, that's the group that will be maintained for a long while.

"Furthermore, when the manager gets fired there's not going to be the upheaval in the organization that occurs now."

Maddon added now when the manager is let go it becomes an entirely different organization with gloom on the other side of it.

"When the philosophy I'm talking about is embedded in the organization you're not going to bring someone in and operate in an entirely different manner. The new manager is going to have to fit into the structure."

John Hart, longtime general manager of the Cleveland Indians and Texas Rangers, now an analyst for the MLB Network, isn't certain the era we're accustomed to is truly passing us by.

"Could be, but I'm not sure," he said. "I like some of the new guys who're managing.

"The Mike Mathenys and John Farrells, the guys obviously who were in the 2013 World Series. They've been impressive."

Hart agrees, though, they both worked closely with their general managers throughout the season.

"The real question is can they do it for a long length of time?" he asked.

Even operating in what might have been the old-fashioned way, Cox, La Russa, and Torre might not have had the types of relationships with the front office Maddon describes, but they obviously worked well with their bosses.

Each was fired at least once, but became more successful the second or third—or in Torre's case, the fourth time around.

Pittsburgh manager Clint Hurdle was at the Winter Meetings in Buena Vista, Florida, in December 2013 when the election of La Russa, Torre, and Cox was announced.

"I was standing in the rear of the room and when I saw them go up on the stage and sit down I felt like a six-year-old kid," he said. "The game was impacted by these men, lives have been impacted by them in such a positive way. How great is our game to have the opportunity to put all three in the Hall of Fame at the same time, to share the honor together—to honor one another?"

Is it the end of an era?

"Time will tell. It very well could be," Hurdle said. "All I know is seeing those men reminded me back when I was a young manager and I'd warn my players, 'I'll guarantee you one thing. You're going to have to play very good tonight because I'm going to get out-managed by that guy over there,' whether it was Lasorda, Torre, Cox, or La Russa.

"The one thing each one will tell you is that they got opportunities. It wasn't one opportunity. They used their eyes and ears. They had a passion for the game. And all were proactive in different areas."

Leyland and Piniella should be the leading candidates for the Hall of Fame when the next election for their work is considered in December 2016.

Leyland may have the edge over his rival because he took teams to the World Series three times. He directed the Florida Marlins to their seven-game championship over the Cleveland Indians in 1997.

Leyland, who retired from the Detroit Tigers after the 2013 season, managed 22 years compiling 1,769 victories.

Leyland, who remains with the Tigers organization as an adviser to CEO/president Dave Dombrowski, turned 69 on December 15, 2013.

He said he retired "because the fuel in my tank was starting to get low. It's time to go."

He has the third most wins as a manager in Tigers history and the 15th highest victory total in major league history.

Piniella, on the other hand, during his 23 years turned franchises around as he lifted the Cincinnati Reds, Seattle Mariners, and Chicago Cubs to the postseason.

"Sweet Lou" has the second-most wins (1,835) of any manager not in the Hall of Fame. He went to the postseason seven times and had the edge over Leyland in 1990 when the Reds eliminated the Pirates in six games of the National League Championship Series.

Even though Piniella took teams to the postseason seven times, the fact that his only World Series appearance was the four-game sweep of Oakland in 1990 could cost him votes.

Again, it seems extremely unlikely any future Hall of Fame manager will come close to equaling the achievements of La Russa, Cox, and Torre.

All three managed in both leagues, even though Cox spent 25 of his 29 years with the Braves and at one time won a world-record 14 consecutive division championships. He won just one World Series, a six-game conquest of Cleveland. It was the Braves' first championship since 1957, giving the franchise three titles in three different cities—Boston, Milwaukee, and Atlanta. Tom Glavine, World Series MVP, won two of the four games.

La Russa split his 33 seasons—17 in the American League with the Chicago White Sox and Oakland, and the last 16 with the Cardinals.

For Torre, his fourth stop, with the Yankees, changed his life and punched his ticket to Cooperstown. He had managed 14 years in the NL with the Mets, Braves, and Cardinals.

When George Steinbrenner hired him on November 2, 1996, he was the Boss' third choice behind Sparky Anderson, Tony La Russa, and Davey Johnson, and the beginning of an historic 12-year run.

He took the Yankees to the postseason each of those years, to the World Series as AL pennant winners six times, and cemented his presence there by winning the Series four of the first five years on the job. His teams won the championship three consecutive seasons beginning in 1998.

The Yankees were 1,173–767 under Torre. It was one of the most dominant stretches in baseball history.

Overall, he won 13 division titles—10 in the rugged AL East for the Yankees, including nine consecutive titles beginning in 1998. He won a division for the Braves and two for the Dodgers, where he managed after he left the Yankees. He finished his career with the Dodgers in 2010, leaving after grooming Don Mattingly as his successor.

In 1996 and 1999, Torre won head-to-head World Series battles with Bobby Cox, as the Yankees defeated the Braves for the title.

Even though Torre became the highest-paid manager in baseball history when his Yankees' contract paid him $7 million annually, he added enormous amounts by taking teams to the postseason.

Shares from the Yankees' World Series and postseasons totaled $1,719,135 for Torre.

Torre, unlike La Russa and Cox, was an All-Star player during an 18-year career in which he had a .297 lifetime batting average. When he won the NL batting title with a .363 average in 1971, he also won the league's MVP award.

Joe's No. 6 uniform number will be joining the retired numbers of Babe Ruth, Joe DiMaggio, Mickey Mantle, and Yogi Berra at Yankee Stadium during the summer of 2014. Derek Jeter's No. 2 is the only number below 10 still in use.

While Torre collected the most championships, when the Cardinals won the 2011 World Series over Texas, in seven games, it was the swan song for La Russa, allowing him to leave the game while on top.

It was his second championship for St. Louis to go with the 1989 title he won when his Oakland A's swept the Giants in the "Earthquake Series."

He also guided the A's to three AL pennants (1988–1990) in 10 seasons, and the Cardinals to three NL pennants.

Tony also spent eight seasons managing the White Sox, taking them to the AL Championship Series in 1983.

There was a thread of success that weaved through the careers of each of these managers.

Cleveland's Terry Francona, 2013's American League Manager of the Year, said: "First of all, longevity is one of the true keys to their successes. They've had the ability to adjust to whatever surroundings they were in. All three moved around, but they were able to adjust to the surroundings and to their personnel. They didn't change their personalities. And that made them extremely successful."

Torre was out of work in 1995. He'd been fired from his third team, the St. Louis Cardinals. He was 55 years old, had a losing record of 894–1,003, and not one postseason series victory. He'd spent more games over a lifetime of playing and managing without ever getting to the World Series than any other man in baseball history.

Wanting to win a World Series, and being unable to achieve it, nagged at Joe.

"I always felt that was something I wanted to accomplish," he told me. "After I was fired from my second or third job—I'm not sure which one—you lose a little heart.

"That's when my wife, Ali, asked me, 'Joe, how do you want to be remembered?' I said, 'Somebody who really never reached what he was looking for.'

"That's when Ali shot back and said, 'What, are you dead?' That was pretty inspirational right there."

The late Arthur Richman, a baseball lifer and an adviser to owner George Steinbrenner, asked Torre if he was interested in becoming the Yankees manager.

According to *The Yankee Years*, a 2009 book written by Torre and *Sports Illustrated's* Tom Verducci, Joe's reply was quick: "Hell, yeah."

Only 10 days earlier, Torre had interviewed for the general manager's job with the Yankees, but he had no interest in such an aggravation-filled job at its $350,000 salary, a $150,000 cut from what he had been earning as manager of the Cardinals before he got fired in June.

The book details his steps to the greatest job he'd ever hold: "His brother Frank Torre did not think managing the Yankees was worth the hassle, either. After all, Steinbrenner had changed managers 21 times in his 23 seasons of ownership, adding Buck Showalter to the bloody casualty list by running him out of town after Showalter refused to acquiesce to a shakeup of his coaching staff.

"It didn't matter to Steinbrenner that the Yankees reached the playoffs for the first time in 14 years, even if it was as the American League wild card team in a strike-shortened 1995 season. Showalter's crimes in Steinbrenner's book were blowing a two-games-to-one lead in the best-of-five Division Series against the Seattle Mariners, resisting coaching changes."

Joe's older brother, Frank, a former major leaguer asked, "Why do you want this job?"

Joe Torre's reply: "It's a no-lose situation for me. I need to find out if I can do this or not."

There was a lot of negativity to Torre's hiring in New York. In fact, Steinbrenner didn't even attend the Yankee Stadium press conference for the announcement.

Torre was gifted in his ability to motivate his players, and in his calmness. The fact that he was a ferocious competitor didn't show on the outside, but it burned on the inside. Joe was a skilled tactician at handling the difficult, demanding New York media.

This gave comfort to the players because he was the buffer between the media and the fragile egos in the clubhouse.

"Mr. Torre is like a second father to me," said All-Star shortstop Jeter. "I learned so much from him, but what sticks with me the most is the way he treated everyone with respect and fairness."

In February 1996, I was at the Yankees new Legends Field spring training complex as Joe put on the pinstripes for the first time, the beginning of this unbelievable era.

When he assembled his first team for Spring Training in 1996, at the very first meeting he told the gathering he'd never won a

World Series (as a manager): "All of my coaches have been to the World Series. That's what I want. But I don't want to win just one. I want to win three of them in a row. I want to establish something here that's special. I don't want to sacrifice principles and players to do it one time. I want to establish a foundation to be the kind of ballclub that is going to be able to repeat."

According to *The Yankee Years*, Dick Williams, who would be elected to the Hall of Fame in 2008, pulled Torre aside after the meeting and told him, "That was a helluva meeting, one of the best I've ever seen."

Pitcher David Cone said: "I remember right off the bat the calming influence that he had, the way he conducted team meetings, the way he talked to people. You could sense that he was going to be a calming influence. He had a lot of experience."

As *USA TODAY*'s baseball editor-columnist, spending a few hours each spring with Torre became a ritual.

We'd usually sit in the dugout and talk about the previous season, his successes with the Yankees and, yes, his relationship with Steinbrenner.

Bill Madden, the *New York Daily News* columnist who wrote the best-selling book *Steinbrenner: the Last Lion of Baseball*, related an interesting moment which set the stage early for Torre's relationship with the always impatient Boss.

Wrote Madden: "Early in the 1996 season, the Yankees had an off-day and Steinbrenner called Torre from Yankee Stadium, chastising him for not taking part in a meeting of his baseball operations people.

"'Here we are, working on things to help make the club better for you, and you're out there in the woods somewhere,' Steinbrenner complained, to which Torre replied: 'I can't believe it, George. How did you know my ball was in the woods? I haven't been able to keep it in the fairway all day.'"

The Yankees, of course, went on to win the World Series in 1996 as Torre beat the Bobby Cox–managed Braves. It was the Yankees' first World Series championship since 1978.

The Torre years were off to a smashing start.

Torre had done a marvelous job—and finally reached his World Series goal.

"I always obsessed about a World Series," he said. "And I remember Ali saying after winning in 1996 and reaching that goal, 'Let's go retire.'

"And I said, 'Let's see if we can do it again.'"

That's exactly what he did—three more times!

As the Yankees were en route to their sweep of San Diego in the previous October's World Series, life was so good for Torre he remarked to his wife, Ali: "Why are all these good things happening to me?"

Then, after he learned he had cancer, he says life was put in perspective.

On March 18, 1999, Torre underwent prostate cancer surgery.

"Somebody said you've got bad luck, blah, blah, blah. You've got cancer," he related to me. "I said, 'Well, it has to happen to somebody. Why shouldn't it be me?' So many good things have happened to me I can't question this."

Torre recovered fully.

Yet, as happy as George Steinbrenner was with winning, I don't think he ever gave Joe the credit the manager deserved.

Frequently, I'd do an interview with Steinbrenner and mention Torre. The Boss would quickly relate Torre's losing record before he got his opportunity with the Yankees. I doubt Steinbrenner ever realized how important Torre was to what became one of the greatest eras in Yankees history.

In October 2007, in a newspaper interview, Steinbrenner threatened to fire Torre if the team did not advance beyond the first round of the playoffs. The Yankees were eliminated by the Cleveland Indians in that round and Torre's departure was on the horizon.

With Steinbrenner's health failing, the Torre years finally came to an end after that season when the Yankees offered him a one-year $5 million contract—a 33 percent pay cut.

To sweeten the deal, several $1 million bonuses were offered if Torre reached certain goals in 2008. To him that was insulting.

"I don't need motivation to do what I do," he told the Yankees. "You have to understand that."

So, Torre moved on.

When he took over the Yankees in 1996, they hadn't won a World Series in 18 years. What he did was reel off an incredible run and now he's in the Hall of Fame.

"I was incredibly fortunate to have played and coached for Joe," said Joe Girardi, who succeeded Torre in 2008. He played under Torre (1996–99) and was his bench coach in 2005. "I learned so many nuances into managing from him.

"The first thing I think of is how much of an importance he placed on developing and cultivating relationships. Not only with players, but with everyone he came in contact with. It's something that was the bedrock for his success."

Andy Pettitte, whose pitching was integral to Torre's success, said: "He was the pulse of all those championship teams. The one thing about Joe is that he never panicked, and that type of calm demeanor allowed us to go out and do the things we were capable of doing. He was a great teacher and father figure to all of us."

George Steinbrenner did not live to see Torre make it to the Hall of Fame. He died on July 13, 2010.

His son, Hal, now managing general partner of the Yankees talked about Torre's era and how important he was to the franchise.

"Joe led our team during one of the most successful runs in our storied history, and he did it with a quiet dignity that was true to the Yankee way," said Hal Steinbrenner. "Joe's place in Yankees history has been secure for quite some time and it is appropriate that he now gets to take his place among the greats in Cooperstown."

Just when it appeared Bobby Cox was going to lift the Braves out of baseball's doldrums, the players went on strike in 1981 and the optimistic outlook built the season before went down the drain.

So did Bobby's early career in Atlanta.

The fifth-place finish cost him his job. In 1980, the Braves had finished above .500 for the first time since 1974. But when impatient maverick owner Ted Turner, at a press conference following the Cox ouster, was asked who was on his short list for manager, Turner said: "It would be Bobby Cox—if I hadn't just fired him. We need someone like him around here."

It took four years, but Turner not only got somebody like Bobby Cox, he got the real McCoy.

After four successful years with the Toronto Blue Jays, Cox returned to Atlanta in 1986 as general manager and in June 1990 fired Russ Nixon, "hired" himself as manager, and returned to the dugout.

As GM, he had spent four successful years bringing aboard talented players such as Tom Glavine, Ron Gant, Steve Avery, Pete Smith, and David Justice. He had the first overall pick in 1990 and tapped a youngster named Chipper Jones.

During his four years under future Hall of Fame GM Pat Gillick in Toronto, Cox lifted the Blue Jays to the 1985 AL East title that earned him the first of four Manager of the Year Awards, but when Turner came calling, Bobby returned "home."

After a quick shakedown cruise with the Braves, Cox began one of the most successful stretches in baseball history.

He and GM John Schuerholz combined for an incredible run of 14 consecutive division titles and a World Series championship in 1995.

Cox, now 72, retired after the 2010 season with the 2,504 wins and 4,508 games managed

And 161 ejections!

Bobby Cox getting kicked out of games was legendary. He's the only manager—or player—to be ejected twice from a World Series game. Folks make light of his battles with umpires, but this really tells much about Cox, the manager. He supported his players to the brink—or ejection.

Atlanta Journal-Constitution reporter David O'Brien relates this story:

Outfielder Jeff Francoeur was in a battle with an umpire in a 2006 game. Cox raced onto the field to back his player. Both Francoeur and Cox were ejected.

Francoeur recounted this to O'Brien:

"I'm like, 'What do I do?' Francoeur asked Cox. Bobby said, 'Go have a couple cold beers and get in the cold tub or something and relax. And then you'll probably have to write a $500 check. Or you can do what I do, write a $10,000 one and tell them when it [money] runs out, let me know.'"

When asked about his election to the Hall of Fame, Cox said: "They say when you're voted to the Hall of Fame your life changes. And it has. I've got goose bumps and it's the greatest honor that we could ever have."

Two days after his December election, Cox sipped on a cup of coffee early one morning and seemed tremendously at peace with himself.

"My life has changed," he said, with a slight twinkle in his eyes. "It's just a wonderful feeling. I'm so blessed."

Torre's amazing career managing the Yankees was the clincher for his election, but it should be mentioned that when Turner fired Cox after the 1981 season, Joe was hired to manage the Braves.

The Braves won the NL West title in 1982 and finished second in 1983 and '84 under Torre. In '84, they slipped to 80–82 and Joe was fired after the season.

Former big-league manager Pat Corrales, with Cox for 17 years and as his bench coach for 10, said "95 percent of the time Bobby didn't need any help. He was just an outstanding manager. He treated his players as human beings. He's always been one of my favorite guys.

"Year in and year out, John Schuerholz would make changes on the team, freshen it somewhat, and it never bothered Bobby. He loved his players and always stood behind them. He deserved this honor."

Cox signed with the Dodgers and while in their system in the minor leagues was helped by Tommy Lasorda, who would himself become a Hall of Fame skipper.

"He never made it to the majors with the Dodgers," said Lasorda. "You know, managers in the Hall of Fame is quite a fraternity. Baseball has been around for over a hundred years and with these three guys, there are only 23 managers in there. It's a tough fraternity to make. All three of them are well-deserved.

"I knew Bobby before anyone knew him. He was a third baseman and I helped him a lot. The thing I remember most is he always had the respect of his players."

Former GM Hart believes players loved playing for Cox and the others because of respect and character.

And it was those qualities that vaulted Bobby, Joe, and Tony to the ultimate stop in baseball's long journey.

I believe there was also a strong thread that tied each of these managers together.

Hart says it was a theme.

"They all shared common themes," he said. "These are guys that have tremendous character and integrity. If you look back at their long careers some were great players, some have climbed up the long, hard road, but you don't stay in that job and have that success without having great character."

The human element?

"Absolutely. That's what the players relate to—whether they like you or don't like you, whether you play them or don't play them, they respect the character. That's been the standard all have exhibited. On top of that, each in his own way has have been true to their own code as to how they want to be baseball people. Bobby was different than Tony, Joe was different than Tony; they all had different ways to get there.

"Yes, I think the common theme is great character.

"You don't have the success they had without the players buying in. The other piece, is as a manager you are working for an organization. You're working for a general manager, for an owner. Ultimately, all of these guys have demonstrated a phenomenal loyalty to the people that they have been with. That's why these guys have kept getting jobs because they understand it might not always be what they want. It might not always come their way.

At some point the organization might say, 'We cannot afford that player, we can't do that.'"

"If you're going to be in the game you have to keep getting contracts."

———•———

In George F. Will's extraordinary 1990 book *Men At Work: The Craft of Baseball*, the author stated, "the meticulous preparation, minute observations and aggressive strategies have made Tony La Russa of the Oakland Athletics the model of the modern-day manager."

Leyland, La Russa's third-base coach for four years (1982–85) while Tony was managing the Chicago White Sox, says, "I've never known anyone who prepares more for a game. He taught me so much."

In 1990, *Sports Illustrated* did its cover story on La Russa, mostly about his preparation and evaluation of players. Tony was a long way from the Hall of Fame then, but the example of his work ethic gives a glance on what helped him get there:

> *At 1:30 in the afternoon on a muggy spring Monday in Boston, the Oakland Athletics are working on their data base. Tony La Russa, the Oakland manager, and three of his aides are working in the small, spartan office used by the visiting team's manager, just off the larger but still cramped room where the team dresses....*
>
> *This day, in Boston, the manager is seated at a metal desk dreary enough to be government issue. He is wearing socks but no shoes, jeans but no shirt and a frown of concentration. On the desk is* The Elias Baseball Analyst. *With La Russa are Lach, Dune and Schu.*

After a fourth-place finish in 1991, La Russa led the A's to a fourth AL West crown in five years, and earned his second Manager of the Year Award in Oakland (the first came in 1988).

Oakland posted a 798–673 record under La Russa's watch from 1986 to 1995, a .542 winning percentage. La Russa is responsible for paving the way to Pittsburgh for Jim Leyland, who managed the Pirates from 1986 to 1996.

"The best lesson Tony taught me was to make sure you have your players prepared every day to play," said Leyland, who remains close friends with La Russa. "That's a tough thing to do when you play 162 games. It's not that easy, but he always did that very well. His teams were always ready to play. That's one of the most important things to managing."

Tony credits Paul Richards with first inspiring him to believe he could succeed as a major league manager.

Originally signed by the Kansas City Athletics as an amateur free agent on June 6, 1962, Tony made it to the major leagues the following year. But after hitting only .199 for an assortment of teams, was released by the Cubs in April 1973. "I was mediocre at best," he says.

After coaching and managing in the minor leagues, and one season in the majors, when the White Sox fired Don Kessinger with a 46–60 record two-thirds of the way through the 1979 season, Tony was named manager.

He was named American League Manager of the Year in 1983, when his club won the AL West but fell to the Orioles in the AL Championship Series.

The White Sox fired La Russa after the club got off to a 26–38 start in 1986, but in less than three weeks the Athletics, the team that originally signed him as a player, called him to take over as manager.

"The stupidest thing I ever did was letting Tony get fired," says White Sox owner Jerry Reinsdorf.

Tony led the A's to three consecutive World Series appearances from 1988 to 1990. After the 1995 season, he left and succeeded Joe Torre as skipper of the St. Louis Cardinals.

It has been nearly 20 years since La Russa moved from Oakland to St. Louis, but as veteran *San Francisco Chronicle* baseball writer John Shea says, "he left a mark on the A's that won't be forgotten or maybe recaptured. It's a big reason he's going to the Hall of Fame."

La Russa, like Torre, remains involved in baseball as an executive on Commissioner Bud Selig's staff. He's also deeply committed, along with his wife, Elaine, to the Animal Rescue Foundation they founded years ago.

Because Tony saw the writing on the wall as a player, he earned a law degree from Florida State University in 1978 and was admitted to the Florida Bar in 1980. About practicing law, he said once, "I decided I'd rather ride the buses in the minor leagues than practice law for a living."

But prior to graduating from law school, he discussed his plans with professors about what he wanted to do in the future. He told them he had an opportunity to coach in the minor leagues and asked what he should do.

La Russa's professor responded, "Grow up, you're an adult now. You're going to be a lawyer."

As he looks back, La Russa told me keeping it simple and remembering the game is a competition is the most important thing.

"The reason you put a team together is to play against another team. You keep score. And the way that works is the organization. If there was one thing that I was taught growing up in the Kansas City organization years ago, it's about the whole organization. I've said it many times, I was so fortunate—Chicago White Sox, Oakland A's, St. Louis Cardinals. If you want to win, you have to have it together—everybody coordinated and just have it go your way."

La Russa and Leyland became friends when they managed against each other in the minor leagues. In 1982, Leyland joined Tony as the White Sox third-base coach.

He kept the job for four years before the Pirates tapped him.

"I was managing in the Instructional League for the Tigers when they hired me in the fall of 1981," said Leyland. "They took me to the World Series, the Yankees and Dodgers, and introduced me. From that moment on, Tony and I have been the best of friends. He was very influential in my career—promoted me pretty good. Tony always believed in me. We've talked a lot of baseball over the years."

Leyland won Manager of the Year Awards with the Pirates in 1990 and 1992.

"Tony was what I call a complete manager," he said. "His expertise was in all areas as well as handling people, and getting the most out of his players. He always had his plan on what he wanted to do in each and every game. He wasn't just about home runs or stealing bases. He did whatever his club dictated, depending on the type of club he had. They always say good managers are thinking two or three innings ahead. Well, he was one of those. But, and this is important, he was able to adjust on the fly. That was so important."

For all the years I've known La Russa, it's difficult to remember him taking credit for his teams' successes.

He's always stressed that his personal success is the product of numerous personal influences. There was hometown Tampa native Al Lopez, a Hall of Fame manager, longtime Cardinals coach and instructor George Kissell, manager John McNamara, pitching coach Dave Duncan, and many, many others.

Ah, yes. Dave Duncan—or "Dunc," as Tony calls him. He has stood by Tony's side, beginning in 1983 as his pitching coach in Chicago, Oakland, and St. Louis.

"He had a great ability to separate every day as if it were something special," said Duncan. "You know, with most people every now and then, you have a bad day and aren't into what's going on. That never happened with Tony. It was like a relentless pursuit of perfection on daily basis."

"We all know the way I managed most teams in Oakland," La Russa told John Shea. "I told them what time the game started and who we were playing. That was it. They were quick-button teams. They had everything."

To that, Dave Stewart, his ace pitcher in the early years, said: "Tony always said he didn't do much with us, and that's such an understatement. A lot of managers couldn't do what he did."

Said La Russa, "I never had a bad day, and I always had a good situation. I don't know any other manager who can say that."

So, we're standing back, watching this magnificent era of managers pass by—all 7,558 wins, the eight World Series titles, the century of work. I don't think any of them are geniuses. They didn't always outthink their opponents, but they always out-worked them. Their strategy wasn't like a computer printout, but they seldom got out-maneuvered. Their determination to win was as relentless as it was fierce.

Joe Torre, Bobby Cox, and Tony La Russa defined the greatness of an era—and era unlikely to be seen again.

9

The Legacy
of Jackie Robinson

Presidents have historically phoned sports figures to congratulate them on outstanding, record-breaking achievements.

On the night the 50th anniversary of Jackie Robinson
breaking baseball's rigid color barrier was celebrated at Shea
Stadium on April 15, 1997, I sat alone with Bill Clinton in a small
room.

If Clinton had been in office that historic day in 1947 and
phoned Robinson, what would he have said?

Clinton, recovering from a leg injury suffered at the home of
golfer Greg Norman, took an unusually long time to answer.

"First of all, I would thank him," said Clinton. "Even then
people knew this was something big—even people who didn't
fully understand the implications of it. Secondly, I would have
commented not simply on his baseball skills, but also on the
character, the dignity, the determination and the willingness to
endure the rejection—all the things blacks went through.

"It took much more than athletic skills to get where he was.
Even after Jackie Robinson, Willie Mays was turned down in
Boston before he came to New York with the Giants.

"This was an enormous reflection of Jackie's character and his inner self-confidence that he was willing to do this."

As the decades have passed, what Jackie Robinson did in 1947 for baseball made America *more* America.

With untold courage at that time, he ended decades of baseball segregation and cracked the Brooklyn Dodgers lineup in what had been an all-white sport.

I believe Jackie summed it up best: "Life is not a spectator sport. If you're going to spend your whole life in the grandstand just watching what goes on, in my opinion you're wasting your life."

He didn't waste his time—or his life. He carried the hopes of black people on his shoulders every day. Had he failed, many would have seen that as the race failing.

I'll amend that: Jackie Robinson carried the hopes and dreams of every right-thinking American.

Consider:

It happened the year before President Harry S. Truman desegregated the U.S. Armed Forces on February 2, 1948. Strong steps were taken to eliminate discrimination in the armed services.

It was seven years before the Supreme Court's 1954 *Brown v. Board of Education* decision forcing school integration.

And 17 years before landmark civil rights legislation—the Civil Rights Act of 1964 was enacted on July 2, outlawing major forms of discrimination against racial, ethnic, national, and religious minorities, as well as women.

In a sense, Robinson foreshadowed the major civil rights movements of the 20th century.

It was a seminal point in the way people felt about black Americans.

I was 11 at the time and vividly remember my dad, a bank president who considered himself a champion for minorities, trying to explain to me how important this moment was—even though it was just on the baseball field—for our country as a whole. At school the next day, in my all-white classroom, my baseball-crazed friends were abuzz with talk of the first black player in Major League Baseball.

Attitudes changed and the doors swung open for other players.

Three months later, Larry Doby became the first African American in the American League when he signed a contract to play for Bill Veeck's Cleveland Indians.

Others, who would become greats of the game and ultimately land in the Hall of Fame followed—Roy Campanella, Don Newcombe, Monte Irvin, and Willie Mays.

A first full season (1996) had passed since the players' strike of 1994–95 when Major League Baseball planned to honor the 50th anniversary of Robinson's historic event.

Leonard S. Coleman Jr., then National League president and the highest-ranking African American in professional sports, was in charge of the celebration at Shea Stadium, closest ballpark to Ebbets Field, where Jackie Robinson played his first big-league game.

"I was trying to think of what we should do," Coleman, long-time chairman of the Jackie Robinson Foundation, remembered. "I was on the Garden State Parkway's Driscoll Bridge, driving to New York. It was like a lightning bolt hit me—retire his number from the entire game.

"It was almost like a divine message coming directly to me. Retire number 42 throughout all of baseball."

Coleman recalls calling Richard Levin, MLB's public relations vice president: "He thought it was a great idea."

Coleman convinced Selig, who received overwhelming support of several team owners.

Not a better gesture could have been imagined; it will forever be a reminder of Jackie Robinson's monumental contribution to our national pastime.

A few hours before the number was retired at Shea that night, I asked Jackie's widow, Rachel, why he wore 42.

"As far as I know he was just assigned that number," she said. "There was nothing special about that then. I've been asked the question over and over again."

During the 1997 ceremony, Selig said players already wearing No. 42 would be grandfathered, but from that moment on it would never again be issued.

"It is an important night for America," Clinton told me during our interview. "When Jackie Robinson broke into Major League Baseball it was a milestone—it was a milestone for sports, but also a milestone in the 50-year effort that really began at the end of World War II to change America's attitudes on the question of race. It was not long after that President Truman signed his order to desegregate the military. A couple years after that the first African American players came into pro basketball.

"A whole series of things happened. It is quite appropriate this is occurring the weekend after Tiger Woods shattered all the records at the Masters. It's a great 50-year story of the emergence of African Americans in athletics and in the larger society of America."

Robert Lipsyte and Pete Levine once wrote: "It was the most eagerly anticipated debut in the annals of the national pastime. It represented both the dream and the fear of equal opportunity, and it would change forever the complexion of the game and the attitudes of America."

Coleman said "no question Branch Rickey's signing of Robinson as the Brooklyn Dodgers' general manager, paved the way."

Coleman, who left Major League Baseball after the 1999 season, believes "the other heroic figure in this who doesn't get due-justice was Happy Chandler, the commissioner. As long as Judge [Kenesaw Mountain] Landis was in office there were not going to be black ballplayers. Rickey went to Chandler with his proposal and Happy agreed."

Chandler, a former U.S. senator and former governor of Kentucky, became commissioner in 1945. He later said he couldn't continue to refuse to allow blacks to play in the major leagues after they had fought for their country during the war.

During his tenure (1921–1944), Landis was determined to maintain segregation. His unyielding stance on baseball's color line was an impediment. Landis died on November 25, 1944, at age 78.

The moving ceremony at Shea Stadium on the 50th anniversary in 1997 led to the annual tradition throughout baseball, Jackie Robinson Day.

And in 2009, all players, managers, coaches, and umpires wore No. 42. The practice has continued since then.

The Yankees' Mariano Rivera, the greatest relief pitcher of all time, was the last player to wear 42. He retired after the 2013 season.

If Jackie were still alive—he died October 24, 1972, at age 53—I believe he would be very proud his number has been retired by all teams. Yet, he'd continue to be very determined.

After Jackie left baseball he spent a lot of time trying to open other doors. He was an executive with a major company and helped organize a bank to provide credit for African Americans.

In 1963 he and his family stood with Martin Luther King Jr. at the Lincoln Memorial for the March on Washington, D.C.

Rachel Robinson, Jackie's widow, was at Yankee Stadium on Mariano Rivera Day on September 22, 2013—a remembrance that Rivera is the last player to wear 42.

"I would've loved to have met Mr. Jackie Robinson," Rivera said, speaking directly to Rachel. "But it's a great pleasure and an honor to be the last MLB player to wear No. 42. Even though I never met him, he has been a hero and an inspiration for me. And I thank Mr. Jackie Robinson for that."

While Jackie Robinson is celebrated for changing the social fabric of America, what is often overlooked is how great a baseball player he was. Color aside, he was without doubt a Hall of Famer, an honor he received when inducted at Cooperstown in 1962.

Jackie was elected to the Hall of Fame by the Baseball Writers Association of America in his first year of eligibility. He received 77.5 percent of the vote, with 75 percent needed for election.

I'm certain his percentage would have been much higher had racism not reared its ugly head and tainted some of the BBWAA members' voting.

From the moment Robinson took the field in 1947—he was Rookie of the Year that season—he began a decade of undeniable success for the Dodgers. As a 28-year-old rookie, he batted .297, drove in 48 runs, hit 12 homers and stole 29 bases.

In 1949, he won the National League batting title with a .342 average and drove in 124 runs and won the Most Valuable Player Award.

Between 1947 and 1956, he was the offensive spark as the Dodgers won six pennants and their only World Series while in Brooklyn. He played in six All-Star Games.

I can close my eyes and see him dancing off the base, rattling and distracting pitchers, threatening them with his awesome speed.

He ended his 10-year career (1947–1956) with a lifetime .311 batting average and 137 homers—and stole 197 bases.

The most significant aspect of his brilliant career, though, wasn't a number. It wasn't related to his marvelous athletic ability. It was what Jackie Robinson had to endure on and off the field, the enormous pressure and stress he was under as Major League Baseball's first African American.

Leo Durocher once said, "He was a great competitor who could do it all. He was a great player, a manager's dream…. If I had to go to war, I'd want him on my side."

Jackie Robinson was unmercifully taunted, especially early in his career with the Dodgers. In fact, even before he was promoted from the Dodgers' Montreal minor-league franchise to the parent club, would-be teammates circulated a petition that they didn't want to play on the same field with Robinson.

In his autobiography, *I Never Had It Made*, Robinson says he learned the ringleaders were "Hugh Casey, a good relief pitcher from Georgia; Southerner Bobby Bragan, a respected catcher; Dixie Walker of Alabama; and Carl Furillo…. The ringleaders were called in individually, and Mr. Rickey told each one that petitions would make no difference."

Regardless, Jackie had that hanging over his head when he moved toward the historic moment.

He began 1947 as the Dodgers' first baseman, a move from second base that Branch Rickey thought would help the team the most.

The fact Jackie was in a dreadful slump during the early weeks of the season is often forgotten.

There were two especially meaningful occasions in that first season.

The Philadelphia Phillies were at Ebbets Field early in the year for a three-game series.

"I was still in my slump and the opening game [of the Phillies series] didn't help," he wrote in the autobiography. "Starting to the plate in the first inning, I could scarcely believe my ears. Almost as if it had been synchronized by some master conductor, hate poured from the Phillies dugout.

"'Hey, nigger, why don't you go back to the cotton field where you belong?'

"'They're waiting for you in the jungles, black boy!'

"'Hey, snowflake, which one of those white boys' wives are you dating tonight?'

"'We don't want you here, nigger.'

"'Go back to the bushes!'

"Those insults and taunts were only samples of the torrent that poured out of the Phillies dugout that April day."

It turns out most of the abuse, well-documented over the years, was directed by the Phillies manager, Ben Chapman.

Robinson said, "I felt tortured and I tried just to play ball and ignore the insults, but it was really getting to me."

It's difficult to separate fact from fiction—or even legend.

None is more prominent than the often-mentioned moment involving Pee Wee Reese, the Dodgers' shortstop and captain. Allegedly, during a difficult time for Jackie when the taunting became deafening, Pee Wee walked across the infield grass from shortstop to first base and put his arm around Robinson—a white player from Kentucky and the black player from Georgia.

This scene was also a powerful moment, oozing with drama, in the highly acclaimed 2013 movie *42*.

In fact, in 2005, a bronze statue of Reese, with his arm around Jackie, was unveiled at a minor league ballpark in Brooklyn, not too far from where Ebbets Field once stood.

In *42*, the gesture took place in Cincinnati.

Robinson described it this way in *I Never Had It Made*:

"Reese's tolerant attitude of withholding judgment to see if I would make it was translated into positive support soon after we became teammates.

"In Boston during a period when the heckling pressure seemed unbearable, some of the Boston players began to heckle Reese. They were riding him about being a Southerner and playing baseball with a black man.

"He put his hand on my shoulder and began talking to me. His words weren't important. I don't even remember what he said. It was the gesture of comradeship and support that counted. As he stood talking to me with a friendly arm around my shoulder, he was saying loud and clear, 'Yell. Heckle. Do anything you want. We came here to play baseball.'

"The jeering stopped, and a close and lasting friendship began between Reese and me. We were able, not only to help each other and our team in private as well as public situations, but to talk about racial prejudices and misunderstanding."

Several years ago, during an interview, Rachel Robinson put it this way: "I remember Jackie talking about Pee Wee's gesture the day it happened. It came as such a relief to him, that a teammate and the captain of the team would go out of this way in such a public fashion to express friendship."

At the media session following Reese's 1984 Hall of Fame induction, I asked him about the legendary moment.

He was vague, at best.

"It was Jackie who had the courage, not me," Reese said. "I could feel what he was enduring, all the taunting, the catcalls. I really don't know how he handled it so well. I've been asked so often about it. No, I wasn't the hero; Jackie Robinson was."

Robinson often said he never cared about acceptance as much as he did respect.

"I had to deny my true fighting spirit so that the 'noble experiment' could succeed," he said.

In the beginning, Jack Roosevelt Robinson had a passion for the rights of his people.

Really, it was a passion for the rights of every American.

10

The Dream Is Alive in Oakland

Across the choppy waters of San Francisco Bay the city of Oakland rises out of the fog, almost like a little boy standing in the back of the classroom. *Hey, what about me?* When it comes to cable cars and Tony Bennett lyrics and five-star restaurants, Oakland is merely "the other place" to sophisticated San Francisco.

As Steve Treder once wrote in *Hardball Times*, Oakland is "the supporting player, the sidekick to the area's glitzy, overbearing, egotistical star."

But when talk turns to baseball and its wonderful history, roles are reversed.

Hall of Famers Frank Robinson, Rickey Henderson, Joe Morgan, and Willie Stargell all came from Oakland.

Curt Flood, who changed the very fabric of the game in his fight for players' rights, grew up there, as did Vada Pinson, Lloyd Moseby, Gary Pettis, Jimmy Rollins, Dontrelle Willis, and scores of other major leaguers.

Billy Martin, who played in the majors and gained fame as a manager, was born and grew up in nearby Berkeley. He was one of the most controversial and colorful managers in the game's history.

Pitcher Dave Stewart, who won two games as the A's swept San Francisco in the historic 1989 "Earthquake World Series," grew up in Oakland and remains a favorite son. Stewart, from the moment the Loma Prieta quake struck on October 17, 1989, at 5:04 PM PT, forgot about baseball and for the next 10 days delved into the recovery effort, working around the clock with hundreds of volunteers.

He's never forgotten his roots and continues to donate time and money to charities he's created in his homedown.

And don't forget Bill Russell. The first black coach in the NBA also hails from Oakland.

Since the Oakland Athletic League was formed in 1919, it has produced 61 major league baseball players, 23 professional basketball players, 47 NFL players, and many Olympic gold medalists.

"There was so much spirit growing up there," remembers Morgan, one of the game's greatest second basemen, who was elected to the Hall of Fame in 1990. "Watching those older players from Oakland in the big leagues inspired me.

"Remember, back in those days, baseball was *the* sport. There wasn't much else. People weren't that concerned with basketball or football. Your parents, your father, everybody pointed you in that direction.

"I think obviously because Jackie Robinson had made such an impact, not only on baseball, but on our country, we looked to baseball. My dad played baseball and I was his batboy. Watching Frank Robinson and the others was a tremendous motivation for kids in the area."

Robinson, during an extensive interview with me in December 2013, tried to explain the Oakland phenomenon. "It was like, 'I want to do it too.' It was a chain," he said. "There were a lot of outstanding players, but you had that feeling you wanted to be in the right place at the right time. And, luckily, I was."

Rickey Henderson chewed on the question for a few moments.

"Yes, it was a great time for sports when I was growing up in Oakland—and long before that," he told me during an interview. "Fathers brought the kids out to play. From their generation they loved playing baseball and other sports. To me, they kept sports alive in Oakland.

"Now, the economy has been so bad that we don't have parents taking their kids to play. When I was a kid Mr. Hank Thomas tricked me into playing Babe Ruth baseball. He'd come to my house, get me out of bed, and take me to the ballpark. He'd entice me with a glazed doughnut and a cup of hot chocolate—all that good stuff.

"He was so much in to it; he gave us an opportunity to play sports. He was the father around the neighborhood. He got all the kids together, to the ballpark, and to keep them out of trouble. He gave us a chance to play sports."

Earlier, in the 1920s and '30s, San Francisco produced the premier players, led by Joe DiMaggio, Lefty O'Doul, Tony Lazzeri, Frank Crosetti, and Joe Cronin.

But across the bay, Oakland was becoming more than baseball's best-kept secret. It was sending the likes of Chick Hafey, Lefty Gomez, Ernie Lombardi, Cookie Lavagetto, and Augie Galan to the majors.

Jackie Jensen, who graduated from Oakland High School in 1945, was American League MVP in 1958.

The quality of baseball talent produced by Oakland beginning in the mid-1950s was extraordinary.

In Treder's study, he states: "The explanation of what happened is an intriguing question. Professional sports, baseball included, has always been an attractive pursuit of working-class young men, often children of recent immigrants: note the high proportion of the star players from the Bay Area in the 1920s and '30s with Italian surnames, products of the great Italian immigration to the Bay Area that took place in the 1890 to 1920 period.

"A similar dynamic prompted athletically inclined young Bay Area African Americans coming of age in the 1950s to look toward professional baseball—as a means of economic advancement [as well as excitement, fun, travel and fame—and yes, one might read all these as euphemisms for female attention] in an environment which provided few comparable alternatives."

There was an outstanding coach named George Powles at Oakland's celebrated McClymonds High School in the 1950s. He had an enormous impact on his young players.

Robinson, now MLB's executive vice president for player development, became one of the game's greatest players. Frank, two-time MVP, Rookie of the Year, and a 12-time All-Star, was signed out of McClymonds High in 1953 by the Reds.

On October 3, 1974, Cleveland Indians general manager Phil Seghi named Robinson the team's player-manager, Frank thus becoming the first African American manager in major league history.

Robinson also managed the Giants, Orioles, Expos, and Nationals and was named American League Manager of the Year in 1989.

In many conversations I'd had with Dave Stewart over the years, he often mentioned growing up in Oakland. He'd tell me about playing on fields of the Greenman Field Baseball Complex.

"Joe Morgan and Frank Robinson once played on those fields," he'd say, with that fierce look that was his trademark on the mound. "Guys like Curt Flood and Willie Stargell and Vada Pinson. Those fields were all home to them.

"When you look at the people who've come out of Oakland, I think you can say we really have something to be proud of."

The 1989 World Series matched the A's and Giants, fitting opponents separated by a body of water.

Stewart pitched a five-hit, 5–0 complete-game shutout in the first game at the Oakland Coliseum. The A's won the second game 5–1 and after a day off, the Series was to resume at Candlestick Park.

The earthquake struck the Oakland–San Francisco area with a magnitude of 7.1 just as thousands of fans were filing into the ballpark to watch batting practice.

The destructive nature of the quake was devastating. An hour before it struck, I took a cab from the Hyatt Hotel in Oakland to Candlestick, a route that traveled over the Interstate 880/Nimitz Freeway, a major link to the Oakland–San Francisco Bay Bridge.

That freeway collapsed during the quake, killing scores of people. Sixty-three died as a result of the quake.

Hours after the collapse, Stewart was at the wreckage, lending a hand. He returned day after day until the Series, after a 10-day interruption ordered by Commissioner Fay Vincent, resumed.

Stewart told me he wanted to be there. He owed that to his hometown in this time of need.

"I just stand and watch and try to boost the spirits of those people working all night, the people trying to find bodies and cleaning up the rubble, " he said. "I haven't figured out why I'm drawn here, except that for me this isn't something to gawk at like a tourist. This is part of my life."

He became a hero in Oakland.

It seemed only fitting when the World Series resumed at Candlestick on October 27, Dave Stewart was the winning pitcher in Game 3, a 13–7 rout of the Giants. After the A's, managed by future Hall of Fame manager Tony La Russa, completed the sweep with a 9–6 victory in Game 4, Stewart was named World Series MVP.

Stewart, now an agent, pitched for 16 years and was involved in three World Series championships. A 20-game winner for four consecutive years (1987–1990) for the A's, he pitched for five teams and won 168 games. He pitched a no-hitter against the Toronto Blue Jays on June 29, 1990.

Fittingly, he returned to his hometown and pitched for the A's in 1995, his final season.

Curt Flood attended McClymonds, but graduated from Technical High, the same school that produced Rickey Henderson. He signed with the Reds in 1956. Vada Pinson, also from McClymonds, was also signed by the Reds in '56. McClymonds product Jesse Gonder was signed by the Reds in 1955.

And as far back as 1926, Ernie Lombardi graduated from McClymonds.

"Most of the guys from Oakland went to the same place—the Cincinnati Reds," says Morgan. "I've never been able to determine exactly why, but there was a pipeline to Cincinnati. Robinson, Flood, Tommy Harper, Vada Pinson, Joe Gaines, Jesse Gonder, and some I've forgotten, ended up there."

Powles also coached Oakland's "Bill Erwin Post No. 337" American Legion team which won the national championship in 1949 and 1950. J.W. Porter was the star player.

I turned to the 1951 *Sporting News Baseball Guide* and on page 156 is a photo of the 1950 Legion champions. Freckle-faced J. W. Porter and a tall and gangly Frank Robinson are pictured in the first row.

"For the first time in the 24-year history of American Legion Junior Baseball, a team won the coveted national championship in successive seasons," the story states. "Another record was set by J.W. Porter, Oakland's catcher, when he captured the national batting championship for the second successive year. The 17-year-old receiver, who hit .551 in 10 tourney games the previous year, produced a .488 average in 1950."

The story went on to say that Porter received a $50,000 bonus for signing with the Chicago White Sox and was named the Legion's No. 1 player of the year.

Porter, a graduate of Technical High, played just six years in the majors and never batted above .250.

Treder writes this about Powles: "Clearly the [Oakland] phenomenon was larger than any single individual; something systemic was going on. An infusion of newly arrived families producing hungry, ambitious young men, eagerly embracing great challenges for an opportunity to enjoy great rewards never before available to people like them, combined with a sound economic infrastructure, and a rich baseball culture, produced an explosive burst of baseball achievement."

In 1949 Robinson first met Powles, the legendary coach. Frank didn't turn 14 until August 31 that year, but was excited as the Legion team won the national championship.

"Mr. Powles coached at the high school, McClymonds, that I eventually went to and had the youth teams during the summer,"

Robinson explained. "It was almost automatic to play for him and what a blessing it was.

"You had to be 15 to play Legion ball, but I was just 14 in 1950," he added. "But he let me play. I didn't beg him. He knew talent, I guess. He was always willing to work with kids. He thought enough of me to put me on that club because there were already a lot of outstanding players at that stage of their careers."

Powles' approach was teaching youngsters "how to think baseball."

Robinson says he overcame his shyness and by following Powles' advice was able to become much more confident.

The Legion team again won the national championship in Frank's first year in 1950. The title game was just after Robinson's birthday on August 31. Days after turning 15, he hit a key triple to aid the championship.

"I was on the 1950–1951 teams; I was the youngest player then to ever play American Legion baseball."

Robinson graduated from McClymonds in 1953 and was signed to a $3,500 contract by Bobby Mattick, described as the Cincinnati Reds superscout.

When asked if Oakland provided an exceptional opportunity for African American youngsters, Robinson said that wasn't necessarily the focus.

"It wasn't mostly that," he said. "Mr. Powles, for example, had teams that played on weekends of all mixtures. The Legion team was mostly from the rival high school, Technical."

To Robinson, his beginning in Oakland "was everything to me. It set the stage for my career; it gave me the foundation that I draw from to this day. I take things that Mr. Powles told me and use them every day.

"I never thought Mr. George Powles got his just-due for what he did for the youth and the young people in Oakland," Frank added.

"At that time I didn't even think about it, but he had a great talent to teach the game. He was a minor league player, but never made it to the major leagues. He had that knack to get across his beliefs and make them understandable. Those types of individuals don't come along too often."

Robinson said many times after he became a manager, he'd ask himself, "'How would Mr. Powles handle this?' I drew from the foundation, the information, the things told us—when to do it, how to do it throughout my career."

Pausing a moment, Frank said: "Yet as I was managing I had to be myself and do it the way I wanted to. He told us things I didn't know about until I got to pro ball. I thought I was ahead of the young kids in the Cincinnati organization by acknowledging the wisdom he bestowed on me."

Robinson was 20 when he made his major league debut with the Reds on April 17, 1956. He batted .290 and tied the rookie record with 38 homers, winning the National League Rookie of the Year Award.

He became one of the most feared hitters—and base runners— in the NL for the next 10 years. He won his first MVP Award in 1961 when he hit .323, with 37 homers and 124 runs batted in as the Reds won the National League pennant before losing to the Yankees in the World Series.

His 10th year, 1965, with the Reds was his last.

Even though he hit 33 homers and drove in 113 runs—the best run-producer in Reds' history—owner Bill DeWitt Sr. felt Frank's skills were fading and that he was frequently hobbled by leg injuries.

Robinson was traded to Baltimore for pitchers Milt Pappas, Jack Baldschun, and outfielder Dick Simpson after the '65 season.

"I was devastated," Robinson told me. "I was with the organization that signed me, had put in 10 years at the major league level. I was thinking I'd spend my entire career with the Reds. I was happy and comfortable in Cincinnati. That might have been one bad thing: I was comfortable.

"It took me about a week to get over it. There were some things said about me as to why I was traded, but they weren't true. I knew I could still play the game and the fans knew I could still play. I had a good year in 1965.

"After I thought about it, I said, 'Well, this may be the best thing for me.' Sometimes when you're in one place you get a little stagnant or a little stale. You think you're doing things the way you're supposed to be doing them 100 percent, but you're really not. That was the jolt at the time I needed to bring out my talent the way it should have been.

"After I got over to Baltimore, people said, 'Well, you have something to prove.' I said, 'No.' I knew I could play and all I had to do was go over there and do what I was capable of doing with the talent they had there—Boog Powell, Brooks Robinson, the outstanding pitchers."

His first year, 1966, in Baltimore was one of his finest.

He led the Orioles to the World Series and a four-game sweep of the Dodgers. It was his magnificent Triple Crown season. He led the AL in homers (49), RBI (122), and batting average (.316). He added the AL MVP to his NL trophy and also was MVP in the World Series.

Baltimore lost the 1969 World Series to the Miracle Mets, but in 1970, Robinson was the catalyst for a team that won the AL pennant and quickly disposed of Cincinnati in the World Series.

In 1971, Frank's last in Baltimore, he once again helped the Orioles to the World Series. But it was Roberto Clemente and the Pittsburgh Pirates that prevailed in seven games.

On September 13 of that year, he blasted his 500th home run off Detroit's Fred Scherman; he ended his career with 586.

He finished his Hall of Fame career—he was elected in 1982—playing with the Dodgers, Angels, and finally the Indians, where he made history by becoming their player-manager.

Morgan told me, "I followed in the newspaper many of the players who were playing American Legion ball. That was my first knowledge of Frank Robinson and Vada Pinson. They were a little older than I was. They weren't playing Babe Ruth League when I was.

"Everybody remembers Curt Flood with the Cardinals, but he started with the Reds and got traded to St. Louis," Joe said. "We could go to the park every day and there were people playing baseball. Some of those parks are now used for soccer, some are not used at all. The same networking to get kids to the big leagues isn't available today.

"From my era, Rudy May and I are the only two guys from our school [Castlemont High] that went to the majors."

"Little Joe," as he was called, had his No. 8 retired by the Reds in 1998 and a statue was dedicated in his honor in 2013. He had an outstanding 22-year career, spent mostly with Houston and the Reds.

Morgan's major league career began in 1963 with the Houston Colt .45s before they adopted the Astros name in 1965. During the 10 seasons that Morgan was in Houston he hit 72 home runs and stole 219 bases. In 1966 and 1970 he was on the NL All-Star Team.

In 1971 the Astros traded Joe to the Reds, a trade still considered one of the worst in Astros' history.

His arrival as the second baseman, gave the "The Big Red Machine" an integral addition that would lead to consecutive World Series titles in 1975 and 1976 and earned him back-to-back National League MVP Awards—a first for an NL second baseman.

He was a 10-time All-Star and the Gold Glove second baseman five consecutive years from 1973 to 1977.

Morgan played for the Astros from 1963 to 1971 and the Reds from 1972 to 1979. He returned to the Astros in 1980, and played two years with the Giants (1981–82), one year with the Phillies (1983), and finished his career with his hometown team, the Oakland A's (1984).

He was elected to the Hall of Fame in 1990.

Curt Flood played in the same outfield at McClymonds High School with Robinson and Vada Pinson, but as Frank points out, Flood graduated from Oakland Technical High in 1956 after transferring there.

He began his major league career on September 9, 1956, with the Reds after signing with them in the spring. He played some for the Reds, before being traded to the Cardinals in December 1957.

He was one of the premier center fielders in the majors for 12 seasons, winning seven consecutive Gold Gloves beginning in

1963. When he walked away from baseball to begin his legal battle, he had a career .293 average, 636 runs batted in, and 1,861 hits.

Although Curt Flood, who died January 20, 1997, was an outstanding player, he'll always be known for refusing a trade to the Phillies and challenging Major League Baseball's ages-old reserve clause.

On October 7, 1969, the Cardinals traded Flood, Tim McCarver, Byron Browne, and Joe Hoerner to the Phillies for Dick Allen, Cookie Rojas, and Jerry Johnson.

Flood refused to report to the Phillies, saying they had a dreadful record and played in run-down, ancient Connie Mack Stadium. He called Philadelphia fans belligerent and racist.

I was covering the Phillies at the time and remember a meeting Flood had with Philadelphia general manager John Quinn. Quinn came away from the meeting confident Flood would accept the trade, but added if he didn't he'd lose his $100,000 salary.

Marvin Miller, executive director of the Major League Players Association, met with Flood and told him the union would help fund a lawsuit if Curt decided to reject the trade and pursue his legal options.

At the time, I obtained a copy of a letter Flood sent to Commissioner Bowie Kuhn, dated Christmas Eve, 1969.

It read:

After 12 years in the major leagues, I do not feel I am a piece of property to be bought and sold irrespective of my wishes. I believe that any system which produces that result violates my basic rights as a citizen and is inconsistent with the laws of the United States and of several States.

It is my desire to play baseball in 1970, and I am capable of playing. I have received a contract offer from the Philadelphia club, but I believe I have the right to consider offers from other clubs before making any decision. I, therefore, request that you make known to all Major League clubs my feelings in this matter, and advise them of my availability for the 1970 season.

Flood told the players' union executive board, "I think the change in black consciousness in recent years has made me more sensitive to injustice in every area of my life." He followed that remark by saying he was essentially challenging the reserve clause as a major league player.

The reserve clause (prior to free agency, which came about in 1976) basically binds a player to his team for life unless he's traded or released. Flood was turned down by Kuhn and Major League Baseball, and ultimately appealed his case to the U.S. Supreme Court.

Flood lost his legal challenge, but it brought about a strong united movement by the players as they fought the reserve clause and sought free agency. They eventually won and free agency, which has changed the financial fabric of the game, came about in 1976. Any player with six years' service who is unsigned for the next season can become a free agent.

And then there was "Pops," Willie Stargell, who moved around the country before settling as a teenager in Oakland with his mother. Stargell graduated from Encinal High School, where his baseball teammates included Tommy Harper and Curt Motton.

Willie was signed by the Pittsburgh Pirates in 1958, an organization he would spend his entire 21-year (1962–1982) career with.

Stargell was beloved in Pittsburgh because of his style of play, the swish of his bat in warm-ups, and his mammoth home runs. He'd often warm up in the on-deck circle with a sledgehammer, adding to the intimidation. Before many of the new ballparks were built, Pops held the distance record for homers all over the league.

At Philadelphia's Veterans Stadium, which has now been replaced by Citizens Bank Park, the feared power hitter Stargell crushed the longest home run in the park's history. It was during a 14–4 rout of the Phillies and Jim Bunning on June 25, 1971. The spot where the ball landed in the upper deck in right field was marked with a yellow star with a black "S" inside a while circle.

After Willie died in 2001, the white circle was painted black. The star remained in place until Veterans Stadium was blown apart in the spring of 2004, as part of its demolition.

One of Stargell's brightest moments came in the 1979 World Series when the Pirates defeated the Baltimore Orioles in seven games.

Stargell and his teammates adopted the Sister Sledge hit song "We Are Family," which became the theme for the Pirates and their championship that season.

"When I played, there were 600 baseball players, and 599 of them loved Willie Stargell," said Joe Morgan. "He's the only guy I could have said that about. He never made anybody look bad and never said anything bad about anybody."

Stargell, elected to the Hall of Fame in 1988, batted .282, with 475 homers and 1,540 runs batted in. He helped the Pirates to World Series victories in 1971 and 1979. He died April 9, 2001.

Pirates manager Chuck Tanner said "having Willie Stargell on your ballclub is like having a diamond ring on your finger."

Henderson, an All-America running back at Oakland's Technical High School, dreamed of playing football for the Oakland Raiders. He turned down numerous college football scholarship offers. Instead, he signed with his hometown A's after being drafted in 1976.

As a boy, he became friends with maverick Oakland A's owner Charles O. Finley, who became aware of Rickey's speed and explosiveness.

Henderson made his major league debut on June 24, 1979. He batted .274 and stole 33 bases during the remainder of the season.

In 1980, Finley hired the controversial Billy Martin to manage the A's. Martin installed "Billy Ball" and it was that approach that vaulted Rickey Henderson into the national spotlight. In three of Rickey's first four years he stole 100 or more bases. (The only year he didn't steal 100 was the 1981 season, which was shortened by a 50-day players strike that lasted from June until August. Rickey still managed to steal 56 that season.)

I asked Rickey what it was like to play for Martin.

"My relationship with Billy Martin? He was like a father figure," Rickey said. "He took me in sort of like a son. I think he figured I was the type of player that would go out, run down a wall, or break down some bricks to succeed. He saw that in me because he was that type of player. He always felt I went out to win each and every day."

Henderson said, "I really wanted to play in the NFL before I wanted to play Major League Baseball. My mom decided because I was a little smaller I'd have longevity as a baseball player. So, she chose that I became a baseball player.

"I gave her a few years for me to even get to the majors. And if I didn't make it, I'd go back and be a football player."

Even in high school, Rickey had to be coaxed to play baseball.

"A counselor in high school, a Mrs. Tommie Wilkerson, she got me to playing baseball in high school. When I went there, I played a little basketball, but my sport was mainly football. She didn't have enough players, so she went around the school asking some of the guys to play baseball.

"She bribed me. She would pay me a quarter every time I would get a hit, a run scored, or stole a base. After my first 10 games, I had 30 hits, 25 runs scored, and 33 steals—not bad money for a kid in high school. I'd take the money and go out and spend it on my girlfriends."

Growing up in Oakland, he said, "My heroes were Jackie Robinson, Willie Mays, Hank Aaron, Reggie Jackson.

"Ah, yes, Reggie Jackson!"

Reggie, the future Hall of Famer, played eight years with the A's beginning in 1968. Henderson idolized him.

"I'd stand in the parking lot, waiting for his autograph," Henderson remembered. "I'd say, 'Reggie, can I have your autograph?' He'd pass me a pen with his name on it. He never gave me his autograph!

"But the year I stole 130 bases, Reggie was running after me for my autograph. I told him, 'I can't give you my autograph at this time because I've never had yours!'"

Said another Hall of Famer, Dave Winfield, who was a Henderson teammate when both were with the Yankees: "He was one of the best players that I ever played with and obviously the best leadoff hitter in baseball history."

"He's the best leadoff hitter of all time, and I'm not sure there is a close second," says Billy Beane, current Oakland A's general manager.

"I enjoyed being a leadoff hitter," Henderson said. "I think ever since I was a Little League ballplayer, I always wanted to start the game, be the first to get a hit and first to score a run. The leadoff spot for me was something I enjoyed my entire career.

"Each and every day that I put on a uniform I wanted to win, not just play."

Henderson led off a major league game with a home run a record 81 times. But in nearly 10 times as many cases (796), Rickey started an inning with a walk.

Rickey owns the all-time stolen-base record of 1,406. His single-season mark of 130 steals, set in 1982 when he was with the A's, still stands.

He played for nine teams over 25 seasons. He led the American League in steals 12 times and set all-time records for runs scored (2,295), and unintentional walks (2,129). A 10-time All-Star, he was the American League MVP in 1990 when he batted .325, with 65 steals, 28 homers, and 61 RBI.

"As a kid growing up in Oakland, playing baseball, I just wanted to play the game, but newer knew what I could achieve. I just wanted to have success," he said.

They called Rickey Henderson brash, he calls himself competitive; he says it's all about being a winner.

"When I was inducted at the Hall of Fame, it was a wonderful feeling—I worked hard and played the game right. All I did was worthwhile."

When Rickey was inducted into the Hall of Fame on July 26, 2009, he said: "To all the kids out there, follow your dream, believe in your dream. Dreams do come true. When you think of me, I would like you to remember that kid from the inner city that played the game with all his heart and never took the game for granted."

Harper, Stargell, Jimmy Rollins, and Dontrelle Willis attended Encinal High in Alameda.

Rollins has become one of baseball's premier shortstops since making his major league debut in 2000. He was the National League MVP in 2007, has won the Gold Glove four times, and is a three-time All-Star.

When he was growing up in Oakland, his idol was Henderson, who was with the hometown Oakland A's at the time. He patterned his style of play, his swagger, his demeanor after Henderson.

Rollins, like Henderson, is primarily a leadoff hitter.

Early in Jimmy's career, Henderson told him: "I always tell leadoff hitters they should take more pitches. That makes them more of a threat. Not only that, but by taking pitches, you give your teammates a longer look at the pitchers—what he's throwing, etc. The pitcher is usually going to give the leadoff hitter his best shot."

Henderson has followed and studied Rollins' career closely.

"Growing up in Oakland was special," said Jimmy Rollins. "There was so much history of the great athletes who came from there. The competition was so great.

"In my youth it was always about playing Los Angeles–area sports," he said. "It was almost like we played for the superiority of the state.

"I loved to go down there and play baseball—Northern Cal versus Southern Cal. If you were from Oakland, you figured like you were representing the better half of California. If you were from Los Angeles, you felt the same. That was reflected in all sports, especially baseball."

The Rollins family and Henderson go way back.

"I played with Jimmy's dad in school," said Rickey.

James Sr. was a California weightlifting champion, but says Jimmy owes much of his baseball talent to his mother, Gigi (Gyvonnie).

"She had all the tools," says the elder Rollins. "She taught him the right way and the wrong way to play the game."

Gigi Rollins says "Jimmy's always wanted to be the best at what he does. That's what makes him excel."

Gigi and Dontrelle Willis' mother were outstanding softball players in the Oakland area when they were younger. Now, they're neighbors and visit each other frequently. But it was the father who helped Jimmy become the outstanding fielder he is. He has excellent agility and exceptional range.

"When I was growing up in Oakland, we'd get up early and my dad would take me out to practice," Jimmy says. "We'd go to the roughest field because it was a challenge. He'd always try to find a field that was beat up and let the ball jump around. You catch that ball, and you've got some good hands."

Rollins' father adds, "We'd go to places where there were roots in the ground and the ball would take crazy hops. Then, I'd take him to a smooth field to show him the difference. Then, we'd go back to the rough field, and I'd hit it to him pretty hard so he'd be able to take different spins."

Rollins remembers how rough some of the fields were.

"That's basically what it was then," he said. "A lot of times for us to become better we played on bad fields. That's how we learned. If you go back and see some of the players who had great hands and stuff like that, a lot of them are from Venezuela or Puerto Rico or the Dominican and they played on those types of field. To me, that's what made them better fielders."

Jimmy's dad also taught his son to be a switch-hitter before he was 10.

"I started him out by having him hit only on the left side for a year," he says. "One day he came into the house all crying and everything. He said he couldn't hit from his natural [right] side anymore. I told him not to worry. He thought he'd lost it, but I told him he'd just converted himself over to a switch-hitter."

Rollins' mother says she knew her son, one of three children (his younger brother Antwon was an outfielder in the Texas Rangers organization), had talent when he was just a toddler.

"He was maybe only a year old when I first started rolling the ball to him," she says. "I'd sit on the stairs in front of the house, and I would roll it. He'd pick it up and roll it back to me."

When Rollins was eight, he tried out for an Oakland Babe Ruth League team (for eight- to 10-year-olds), made the A&T Travel team and brought back a black-and-gold uniform, á la Oakland A's.

"He was really mature for his age, yet I thought at eight he was too young for competition. But I said 'Okay,'" his mother recalls. "He played very well. For him, I think it was fortunate he was surrounded by some great players in Oakland. I knew he knew how to play, but he had never played against anyone competitively."

Joe Morgan ended his career in Oakland in 1984.

Dave Stewart returned to play his last season with the A's in 1995.

Rickey Henderson twice returned—in 1989 and in 1998—during his 25 years.

I asked Jimmy Rollins—under contract with the Phillies, the only team he's played for—if he would like to play in his hometown. Maybe end his career there.

"If you had asked me years ago, I would have said no," he replied. "Now, it's something I would consider because it is the team I grew up rooting for.

"I got to see Rickey do it, I got to see Ken Griffey Jr. do it for Cincinnati. Joe Morgan did it.

"If something like that were to ever happen for me it would be a great honor—paying a tribute to a team that inspired me to really want to be a Major League Baseball player."

Thomas Wolfe wrote "You can't go home again." Rollins says when it comes to Oakland he had it wrong.

11

A Kid's Game

L ittle League is truly about the fundamental values of sportsmanship, fair play, and teamwork. Nothing demonstrates the benefits for youngsters from Little League more than an unspectacular game at Dana Point, California, years ago.

Let's just say one of the teams wasn't very good. Awkward is a better word.

Fly balls were being dropped in the outfield, and dropped again when they were thrown back to the infield as the opposing team tore around the bases. A firestorm of hits was inflicted on the losing team.

Run after run crossed the plate. It was hard to watch. Ugly is a better word.

It was the fourth inning and the not-so-good team was down 10–0.

Did someone whisper, "Thank goodness Little League games are just six innings!"

Frank Monzo, coach of the not-so-good team, had used four pitchers and his bullpen was empty.

He turned to his wide-eyed son, 10-year-old Frankie, the catcher, and said, "You're going to pitch the last two innings."

"I don't pitch, Dad," Frankie argued.

"It's for the good of the team," Coach Monzo shot back. "You're my only pitcher."

The little catcher, his head down, moped his way to the mound and finished the game.

His fastball wasn't working, his change-up wasn't changing. Nothing was working. He walked the bases loaded twice.

When the game mercifully ended, the Monzo team was beaten 16–0. And the game wasn't as close as the score!

Later, someone gently asked Frankie Monzo if he felt tremendous pressure going to the mound in the embarrassing blowout.

"No, not at all," he said softly. "Dad, er Coach, told me to go out there and enjoy the moment, have fun, and remember it forever. That's what I did.

"After all, we were out of pitchers and I knew as difficult, and embarrassing, as it was, I could really help the team."

Frankie's dad died a couple of years ago and the former Little Leaguer is now in college, but memories flourish.

"Little League taught me so many lessons and I often think back to that nightmarish moment," he said. "It helped me grow up. Quickly."

Matt Diaz has played in the major leagues for 11 seasons, had a lifetime .290 batting average, and hit over .300 for the Braves three times.

Diaz is quick to point out how important Little League was to him as a youngster, later as he helped Florida State to two College World Series appearances, and then to the rugged major leagues.

He says he's passing along the same lessons he learned to his sons, Nathan and Jake.

"More than anything, Little League teaches kids how to fail," he told me. "In other sports it's somewhat different. In baseball, you cannot hide from failure. It's a huge part of the game."

Diaz adds, "While every player eventually strikes out or is on the losing team, there is always another chance for success in the next at-bat, or the next game."

Charlie Manuel, a former major leaguer, and winningest manager in Phillies history, who led his team to five consecutive division titles (2007–2011) and the 2008 World Series championship, learned that lesson early.

"I was cut from my Little League team in Buena Vista, Virginia," Manuel recalls with a laugh. "Sapp Jones was the coach and he said I couldn't play the game. That was tough to take, but it made me more determined."

Charlie went on to captain his Parry McCluer High School baseball and basketball teams, and after graduation in 1963 was signed by the Minnesota Twins.

"Little League teaches discipline and how to compete at a young age," he says. "It also teaches young people how to play the game."

Little League baseball was important, too, for Joey Jay, a strapping 6'4", hard-throwing right-handed pitcher from Connecticut.

He was 12 years old when Little League teams were formed in his hometown of Middletown. Joey was larger than most boys his age, but too old by rules to pitch. So he played first base.

But after graduating from Little League he became a pitcher, dominating opponents in American Legion baseball and opponents of Woodrow Wilson High School, where he threw three no-hitters.

The Milwaukee Braves signed him after he graduated in 1953, and because he received a $40,000 bonus he was required to remain with the major league team for two years.

He was just 17 when he made his big-league appearance on July 21, 1953, thus becoming the first graduate of Little League baseball to make it to the majors. He pitched two shutout innings in relief that day at Philadelphia's Connie Mack Stadium as the Phillies hammered the Reds 10–0 behind Robin Roberts.

Hundreds of Little League grads have made it to the big leagues since, but Joey Jay will always be remembered as the first.

He pitched 13 seasons (1953–55, 1957–1966), compiling a 99–91 record, with a 3.77 earned run average. With the Cincinnati Reds in 1961, Jay tied for the National League lead with 21 wins and four shutouts. He added a one-hitter that season as he became the first Cincinnati pitcher since Ewell Blackwell in 1947 to win 20 or more games.

The Reds surged to their first NL pennant since 1940, but lost the World Series to the Yankees in five games. That was the summer Roger Maris surpassed Babe Ruth's season home run record of 60 with 61.

The Boones became the first third-generation family in the major leagues; Little League was the beginning for two of those generations. Grandpa Ray Boone's son Bob began in Little League, as did Bret and Aaron Boone. When Ray was still a player it was his wife, Patricia, who became involved in Little League.

Pat Boone was the designated driver. Before she died in 2008, she said how proud she was of her son and grandsons. She told me how she spent hundreds of hours driving children to Little League games and practice. "But I loved every minute of it," she said. "Waiting patiently in Little League stadiums was all part of it. Then, to see them succeed is what it's all about. It really helped them in baseball."

Said Bob: "She was always behind the wheel of the family station wagon."

Jim Leyland, three-time Manager of the Year, who retired from the Tigers after the 2013 season with 1,769 career wins, is a Little League grad.

"I loved every minute of it," Leyland says. "As I look back, Little League is great, but you have to keep it in the right perspective. You have to be careful, if the parents get involved too much it ruins the purpose of what it is. Some think they have the next Mickey Mantle.

"It is a time when kids want to play some baseball, but it's about camaraderie and learning how to deal with people. It's about sportsmanship and competing—winning and losing, learning how to handle both.

"It's a great lesson in life, but I don't take it quite as seriously as a lot of people do."

Little League baseball, not to mention the many other youth leagues, has become a way of life in America.

Little League was not the first youth baseball program. In fact, Little League came along decades after the first organized youth baseball games were played.

In reality, Little League only revolutionized the way kids play baseball.

My friend, Lance Van Auken, the very capable vice president and executive director of the Little League Museum in South Williamsport, Pennsylvania, points out that before World War II, organized youth baseball in the United States (uniforms, umpires, coaches, full catching gear, and something resembling a real ballfield) was confined mostly to "club" teams.

"Any club might have had a feeder system of teenage players and pre-teens who played ball as a way to prepare for the adult team," he says. "The clubs, usually in a city, might have been affiliated with a trade, a fire department, or a service organization. Coaches were paid to lead the teams.

"Then came Carl Stotz. He was a baseball fan, an interest that began during his childhood when he played as a teen at St. John's Lutheran Church in Williamsport [Pennsylvania] in the 1920s."

Stotz had no sons of his own, but he had nephews. Two of them were Jimmy and Major Gehron. The boys, ages six and nine, often came over to see their "Uncle Tuck," and play catch.

There were no organized baseball games for boys their age in Williamsport at that time. If they could get onto a ballfield, the equipment was too big, and the teenagers would shoo them away.

One day in 1938, while playing catch with Jimmy and Major, Stotz stepped on the trimmed back stems of a lilac bush in his backyard and scraped his leg. At first, the boys were concerned, but the injury was not bad. As Stotz nursed his wound, the boys went back to playing catch. It was then that Stotz described having a kind of epiphany, according to Van Auken's research.

Stotz asked if the boys would like to wear real uniforms, to use equipment that was made just for boys their age, and to play on a field that was smaller and more suited to them. He made a promise to create such a program for them.

During that summer, he recruited a few neighborhood boys. He experimented with field sizes, and tried to find equipment (or modify adult equipment) that the boys could use.

By the next year, the first Little League game was played, on June 6, 1939, at a place called Park Point in Williamsport.

It was just beyond the outfield fence at Bowman Field, then the home of the Williamsport Grays of the Eastern League.

Today, it's home to the short-season Class A Williamsport Crosscutters, and is the second-oldest minor league ballpark in the country.

Stotz managed one of the teams in the first game. Jimmy and Major were on his team, sponsored by Lycoming Dairy. They lost the game 20–8, but came back later to win the first league championship.

The program stagnated throughout World War II, but that gave Stotz time to refine the rules. After the end of the war, stories about Little League appeared in national publications, and requests for information poured in.

It's obvious, what made the Little League program different was coaching. Coaches were not paid as they might have been on club-based teams, but they were fathers from within the community—fathers who suddenly had more time on their hands, thanks to the 40-hour work week. Those fathers coming home from the war by the thousands needed a way to get reacquainted with their families, and Little League provided it.

Van Auken adds that Stotz's personal philosophy about kids baseball also took root. He believed that teaching a boy the fundamental values of sportsmanship, fair play, and teamwork— imparted in an organized way by responsible adults—could be values they retained when they became adults.

Eight years after the first game, the first national tournament was played in Williamsport. Stotz traveled around the nation and world, spreading the word. By the 1950s, Little League was being played in every state and several other countries.

Little League became synonymous with youth baseball, and ingrained in American culture. As such, it was not immune to problems that also cropped up in society.

From the very first years of Little League in Williamsport, it had been integrated. In the 1940s, nobody thought twice about African American children playing on the same teams with white players in central Pennsylvania—years before Jackie Robinson's name became a household one as he broke baseball's ages-old color barrier on April 15, 1947.

But in 1955, segregation was the rule in the southern United States.

Van Auken says that in that year 62 local Little Leagues were chartered in South Carolina. Unbeknownst to the folks at headquarters in Williamsport, 61 of those leagues were all white.

The 62nd league, the Cannon Street YMCA Little League, was composed entirely of children of color. That fact also went unnoticed by Little League headquarters, until it came time for tournaments.

"Every one of the white leagues in South Carolina refused to play the Cannon Street YMCA team," Van Auken says. "Little League's response was: If they would not play Cannon Street, the white leagues would forfeit."

They did not play, and they did forfeit. Not only that, they started a youth baseball program of their own—for whites only—that spread throughout the South. Little League lost hundreds of local leagues as a result, but refused to give in and allow local leagues to bar any player because of skin color.

The organization formed by those all-white leagues still exists today, under a different name, although it is no longer legally able to ban children of color.

That left the Cannon Street team with nobody to play. The rules, even now, require a team to play and defeat a team at a lower level before advancing in the tournament.

While Little League would now be inclined to waive the rule in those circumstances, it did not in 1955.

Says Van Auken: "As a consolation, the team was invited to be the guests of Little League at the World Series that year, to stay in the dorms of Lycoming College just like the other teams, and to have meals in the dining hall. But it would not to be able to play.

"It was a bittersweet experience for a group of boys whose skin color led to adults making decisions they could not understand."

It's difficult to correct a glaring wrong, but what I believe was a successful attempt was made even though years late.

In 2002, surviving members of the Cannon Street team were invited to Williamsport once again.

Before the opening game of the Little League Baseball World Series, the team was presented with something that had been denied to them nearly 50 years earlier—the banner that named Cannon Street YMCA Little League as the champions of the state of South Carolina.

And then there was another struggle.

Indirectly, it hit home.

Dallas Green and I have pretty much traveled the same path since the late-1950s—he as a player, manager, and team executive, me as a sportswriter/editor and baseball reporter.

As a disclaimer, we're both University of Delaware graduates and close friends.

So, when he alerted me to a firestorm brewing involving Delaware's Little Leagues, I was forced to listen. At the time, I was sports editor of the *Wilmington (Del.) News Journal.*

Dallas, on the phone, said that he—no, make that his wife, Sylvia—needed some editorial help. Their daughter Kim wanted to play Little League Baseball, but was being barred because of her gender.

But let Dallas tell the story as he did in his 2013 memoir, *The Mouth That Roared.*

"Baseball matters occupied all my time at work (as Phillies farm director then)," Dallas writes. "And back home, the game was the cause of a major family incident.

"I was at Spring Training in 1972 when Sylvia called and told me about the drama unfolding in our hometown in Delaware. [Basically, the same call I received at the *News Journal*]. She said our nine-year-old daughter, Kim, might be facing 'nine men in black robes' pretty soon. I didn't have time for riddles, so I asked her what she was talking about. She said she was referring to the United States Supreme Court.

"It all started when Kim and two of her friends went to Little League baseball tryouts in Eastburn Acres (a Newark, Delaware, suburb), only to be told that girls weren't allowed to play in the league. The girls were upset about being turned away. Kim took it especially hard. She had been a bat girl in the league the year before, biding her time until she felt she was ready to play on a team.

"Sylvia was upset, too. She knew how much Kim enjoyed baseball and had no doubts she could compete with boys her age. If they had given her a chance to participate in tryouts, everyone would have seen that.

"Sylvia conducted a little research and found that a New Jersey judge had ruled a few months earlier that Little League teams there had to accept girls. But other states didn't have the same requirement.

"Sylvia could have just let it go and found another sport for Kim to participate in. But that wasn't what Kim wanted. She had always played baseball with her older brother, John, and didn't understand why she couldn't play on an organized team.

"It turned out that one of Kim's elementary school teachers was very active in the National Organization for Women. She approached Sylvia about pursuing the matter through the courts. The feeling within NOW was that a recently passed federal law called Title IX made it illegal to ban girls from education programs. And I guess they hoped Little League could be considered an education program."

The Greens and Bodleys have socialized for over 40 years and it has always been obvious Sylvia seldom backs down when she feels deeply about an issue, but seldom initiates the controversy. Family is something else.

"Sylvia was never one to get involved in causes, but this situation was different, because the cause involved her daughter's happiness," Green writes. "She publicly voiced her support for an ACLU lawsuit against the league.

"The national media jumped all over the story. Kim appeared on *The Mike Douglas Show* and hit some baseballs in the studio.

When reporters asked me about the situation, I said I supported my daughter's right to play. But I added I felt girls would eventually decide baseball wasn't the game for them.

"The lawsuit hit a roadblock, but the publicity surrounding the issue ultimately motivated Little League to allow girls to play."

As an aside, on January 8, 2011, Dallas and Sylvia Green's granddaughter, Christina-Taylor Green, 9, was shot and killed in the Tucson, Arizona, massacre that also resulted in the shooting of U.S. Representative Gabrielle Giffords.

Christina-Taylor followed in Kim's footsteps. She was the only girl on her Little League team in Arizona. Fittingly, to honor the life of the feisty little girl, a 10-foot statue of an angel has been erected and now stands watch over the Little League ballpark in Oro Valley, Arizona, where she played. The field has also been renamed "Green Field."

"I admire the Christina-Taylor Greens, Kim Greens, and the Pam Postemas [a female umpire] of the world who took chances and served as role models for other girls and women," says Dallas Green.

In a sense, the struggle for girls to be able to play Little League baseball was a seminal event that dovetailed with American culture.

When the first girl played Little League in 1950, it was seen as a novelty. Kathryn Johnston had tucked her hair under her hat, and posed as a boy during tryouts in Corning, New York. She made the team, and revealed her gender before the first game. She played the entire season because, at the time, Little League rules did not specifically ban girls.

Two years later, the rules were changed, and stayed that way until 1974—two years after the Green protest.

That was the year, 1974, that Little League baseball finally gave in. It was being sued in 20 states, underwritten in many of the cases by NOW, to admit girls. It was at the same time the Equal Rights Amendment was winding its way through state legislatures.

Dire predictions of Little League's doom as a result of females being allowed to participate were proven false. At the same time girls were allowed to play on Little League's baseball teams, Little League started a girls-only softball division.

Today, one in seven Little Leaguers is a girl.

According to Van Auken, the peak of participation in Little League came in the late 1990s, when nearly 3 million kids were enrolled.

Since then, a variety of factors have contributed to a decline not only in youth baseball participation, but in many team sports.

"Countering that decline is something Little League has taken seriously," Van Auken says. "The Little League Urban Initiative, for instance, has proven successful in dozens of inner-city neighborhoods as a way to involve the entire family in a healthy activity.

"And looking at the way the game itself is played also is under scrutiny. Keeping kids involved in the game, and not sitting on the bench or standing around, is a goal not only for games but practices as well. Even the way teams are chosen is being re-thought.

"Expanding the program outside the U.S. also is ongoing. In recent years, teams making it to the Little League Baseball World Series have come from decidedly non-baseball powerhouse nations like Poland, Czech Republic, and Uganda."

Little League today remains the world's largest organized youth sports program, with more than 2.2 million children playing ball in 85 countries.

12

Mr. President

Six weeks had passed since the devastating 9/11 terrorist attacks on America when George W. Bush walked to the Yankee Stadium mound on October 30 to throw out the ceremonial first pitch for Game 3 of the 2001 World Series.

It was more than a first pitch.

It was a powerful message that the president of the United States, even with raised alerts for more terror attacks, would appear at sold-out Yankee Stadium and throw a baseball to a catcher, Todd Greene, behind home plate.

When Bush was introduced by legendary public address announcer Bob Sheppard, "USA! USA! USA!" vibrated throughout the stadium.

I could not believe how the mood, which hours before had been so somber, had changed.

The president had not only lifted the spirits of the over 57,000 baseball fans waiting for the Yankees to play the Diamondbacks, but with a national television audience watching, he'd lifted the spirits of America at a desperately needed time.

Baseball has a way of doing that, and as far back as we can remember, presidents have had close ties to our national pastime.

From George Washington to Barack Obama, presidents have shown their love for the game, and baseball has loved its highest-ranking fan.

Baseball has enjoyed the attention of presidents more than any other sport.

Every chief executive with the exception of Rutherford B. Hayes has had some involvement with our national pastime.

It has even been reported that troops under George Washington played a form of baseball while at Valley Forge and that Washington himself liked to play catch with his lieutenants.

Presidential openers began in 1910, when President William Howard Taft threw out the first ball at what was called American League Park in Washington. That was followed by first pitches from 10 additional presidents at Griffith Stadium and RFK until the Senators moved to Texas and became the Rangers after the 1971 season.

As an aside, is it coincidental that George W. Bush, who would become president, was owner of a team that once was the Washington Senators?

Taft began the practice somewhat by accident on April 14, 1910.

Earlier that morning, Taft had been lustily booed at a rally of suffragists, who were campaigning for women's right to vote.

He went to the game as a fan, but American League president Ban Johnson asked him to throw out the first pitch. Taft tossed the ball to future Hall of Famer Walter Johnson and the practice was born.

As legend goes, the next day the ball was taken to the White House, where Taft autographed it for Johnson.

When Jimmy Carter was in the White House, he became the first president in nearly 70 years to not throw a "first pitch" at any major league ballpark.

However, after Carter left office, he and wife Rosalynn were fixtures in front-row seats at Atlanta Braves games. He often took part in the controversial "tomahawk chop," and I vividly remember Carter, wearing a Braves cap, rushing onto the field in 1992 when the Braves won the National League pennant.

Commissioner Bud Selig has a framed copy of President Franklin D. Roosevelt's celebrated Green Light letter to Commissioner Judge Kenesaw Mountain Landis hanging on a wall near his desk in Milwaukee.

In the aftermath of the Pearl Harbor attack and America's entry into World War II, Landis was concerned whether the 1942 season should proceed. Roosevelt wrote, in part: "I honestly feel that it would be best for the country to keep baseball going."

Selig told me, "It was so important to our country that baseball continue during World War II. As you know, I'm a history buff and I look up at that letter often. It tells a lot about baseball and America."

And nearly six decades later, in a sense, on that night at Yankee Stadium, baseball helped keep America going.

Bush, wearing a blue FDNY jacket in tribute to the New York City Fire Department walked briskly to the mound.

"The crowd was chanting USA, USA, USA! It was a very emotional and a very loud experience and something I'll never forget," Bush told me during a 2005 interview in the Oval Office. "Baseball has a way of doing that. Baseball has a way of dramatizing some of the big moments."

High above the façade in center field at Yankee Stadium a torn U.S. flag that was recovered from the World Trade Center, waved in the cool, gentle October breeze. When it was found in the debris, 12 stars were missing.

Not since October 3, 1956, when Dwight D. Eisenhower was at Ebbets Field to throw out the first ball before Game 1 between the Yankees and Dodgers had a president thrown out the first pitch at a World Series.

"No other sport has been so graced by presidential attention," wrote baseball historians William B. Mead and Paul Dickson in *Baseball: The Presidents' Game.*

Bush, however, was the first president to have played Little League baseball and the first to own a major league team, the Texas Rangers, from 1989 to 1994.

For Bush, owning a baseball team "was a dream come true," he told me.

In his book, *Decision Points,* Bush relates how in 1988 he began the process of buying the Rangers.

"Near the end of Dad's [1988 presidential] campaign, I received an intriguing call from my former business partner Bill DeWitt," Bush wrote. "Bill's father had owned the Cincinnati Reds and was well connected in the baseball community. He had heard Eddie Chiles, the principal owner of the Texas Rangers, was looking to sell the team. Would I be interested in buying? I almost jumped out of my chair. Owning a baseball team would be a dream come true. I was determined to make it happen."

Bush put together an ownership group and on Opening Day 1989 was introduced on the field as the Rangers' new co-owner (with Rusty Rose). The deal had been completed on March 18.

The Rangers finished second in 1993, but in 1994, Bush's last as an owner, were in first place in the American League Western Division when the August 12 players' strike ended the season. They were recognized as the division leader.

It was during the Bush regime that the Ballpark at Arlington opened on April 1, 1994.

Carl M. Cannon, writing in *The Atlantic Monthly*, points out that Bush was a Little League catcher and that during a presidential primary debate was asked what his biggest mistake had been.

He deftly replied, referring to his days with the Texas Rangers: "I signed off on that wonderful transaction—Sammy Sosa for Harold Baines."

Baseball remains his true love.

He carries an electronic device that allows him to check scores and progress of games whenever he wants. He scans the box scores every day. I suspect had it not been for the visibility he gained while owning the Rangers he would not have been elected governor of Texas—his springboard to the White House.

I suggested that to him once.

"I don't know. That's a good question," said Bush, who was elected Texas governor in 1994 and remained in office until 2000, when he won the White House. "I do know that being involved with baseball in Texas was an experience that I loved. I really don't know whether it helped me be elected governor, but that's too hard for me to speculate. Part of defining a person's personality is whether or not they're able to have zest for life and an optimism and enthusiasm for the assignment. I had that."

The day Major League Baseball returned to Washington, April 14, 2005, I sat in the Oval Office and talked with Bush about the game and how important it was for the sport to be in our nation's capital.

"I'm a baseball fan and I love great moments in baseball," he said. "Tonight is going to be, for me personally, a great moment in baseball."

During his eight years in the White House, Bush had satellite dishes installed so he could watch a variety of games.

"I still follow the Rangers closely," he said. "The first major league game in Texas I saw was the Astros. I suffered through the 1980 Phillies-Astros playoff, and the 1986 Mets-Astros playoff. I was there [at the Astrodome] when Mike Scott pitched the 1–0 game vs. the Mets. Glenn Davis homered to win it against Dwight Gooden. That was a classic baseball game.

"The greatest game I've ever seen was the 'Texas Heat,' Nolan Ryan vs. Roger Clemens. Rangers win 2–1, Rafael Palmeiro hits a two-run homer with Cecil Espy on first, Jeff Russell closes.

"It's embarrassing to remember all these facts, but I'm a baseball fan. I love great moments in baseball."

Another time at the White House, when Hall of Famers were the guests of honor, Bush said, "I grew up loving baseball. It's a sport that's passed down from dad to son."

Indeed. Bush, of course, is the son of former president/first baseman George Herbert Walker Bush, who captained the Yale nine.

During another visit in the Oval Office, I had been talking baseball for nearly 30 minutes when the first President Bush got up from behind his desk and began rummaging through a drawer.

"Here it is!" he said, pleased after locating the first baseman's mitt he wore while playing for Yale. "It's my McQuinn Trapper."

After putting it on his right hand, he pounded it several times and a broad smile came across his face.

"I used this glove my three years at Yale," he beamed. He played first base at Yale in 1946 and '47, and was captain in 1948.

"Growing up, Dad would take me to see games at Yankee Stadium, which even then was not too much of a drive from Greenwich, Connecticut, where we lived. I was always a Red Sox fan and my brother was a Yankees fan. We'd go to the Polo Grounds and to Ebbets Field once. I just grew up in a baseball family."

He modestly said he was a good player when he was at Yale.

"Well, I was kind of a flashy kind of guy. I knew the position well and liked it. I guess I really wasn't a great player because of my hitting. I was much better as a fielder."

There were vague hints of turning pro after college, but "I would not have been a good big-league player because I wasn't a good hitter.

"Oh, once in a while a scout would get lost and come by— like the time I went 3-for-5 against North Carolina State in 1948. Double, triple, single.

"Yeah, I fantasized like every other kid. Lou Gehrig was my boyhood hero."

To the elder Bush, baseball is a religion in America.

"It's different from the other sports because as a fan you can do two things at the same time. You can be involved in the game from the stands and yet you can be relaxed. Football is more of an on-edge, up-and-down-the-field type of thing.

"I enjoy baseball because I like to think out the different situations and still you have the exhilaration of seeing a fantastic catch or clutch hit or a daring steal or something like that. Baseball has everything."

In 1992, I flew on *Air Force One* with the elder Bush to the All-Star Game in San Diego. We spent much of the flight talking pros-and-cons about the players selected for the game.

Bush would throw out the first pitch.

He spread a newspaper on a huge mahogany table aboard *Air Force One* at 35,000 feet and started going over the All-Stars who would be playing at Jack Murphy Stadium in a few hours.

He admitted he was partial to players from the Texas Rangers because of the obvious connection with his son, then the owner.

He talked about the three All-Star Games he attended as vice-president and the two since moving into the Oval Office.

For me, none will equal the 1981 game in Cleveland. That game signaled the end of the 50-day players' strike and Bush sat in a field-level seat, which is unheard of today.

"I took Carl Yastrzemski to that game on the plane, and it was a great day for me as a ball fan," he said. "I just love being closer to the action. Unfortunately, we cannot do that anymore because of security precautions."

George W., as the Rangers' owner, had fired Bobby Valentine as manger a week earlier.

"Barbara and I really liked Bobby V.," said the elder Bush. "I had to ask George about that. He just said it was a very difficult decision, but they had to do it because I gather there was a little dissension on the team. I didn't know about that, but I wish Bobby well."

Herbert Hoover once said, "Next to religion, sportsmanship is the greatest teacher of morals, and baseball has given this greatest moral influence to our American way of life."

When Don Larsen pitched his storied perfect game for the Yankees against the Dodgers in the 1956 World Series, President Eisenhower said Larsen's achievement "will inspire pitchers for a long time to come."

In fact, not until the Phillies' Roy Halladay threw a no-hitter in the 2010 National League Division Series vs. Cincinnati, had any pitcher come close to equaling Larsen's feat.

Halladay was deprived of a second perfect game of the year when he walked Jay Bruce with two out in the fifth inning. Halladay, who pitched his perfect game on May 29 vs. the Florida Marlins, remains just one of two major leaguers to pitch no-hitters in the postseason.

Eisenhower, who had thrown the ceremonial pitch for Game 1, in a letter to Larsen, wrote: "It is a noteworthy event when anybody achieves perfection in anything. It has been so long since anyone pitched a perfect Big League game that I have to go back to my generation of ballplayers to recall such a thing—and that is truly a long time ago."

The night Jackie Robinson was honored at a testimonial dinner shortly before he was inducted into the Hall of Fame in 1962, President John F. Kennedy said: "He has demonstrated in his brilliant athletic career that man's courage, talent, and perseverance can overcome the forces of intolerance…. The vigor and fierce competitive spirit that characterized his performance as an athlete are still evident in his efforts in the great battle to achieve equality of opportunity for all people."

In 1975, when President Gerald R. Ford accepted a gold pass from Major League Baseball, he added a touch of humor and humility to his acceptance.

"I sometimes wonder if I would have been better off playing baseball instead of football," he said. "The season would have been longer, but I think the doctor bills would have been shorter.

"There are a lot of similarities between baseball and politics. One of the worst things you can hear in baseball is: 'You're out!' Same thing in politics!… Politicians were saying 'Wait till next year' long before baseball fans ever thought of it!"

Once, during a brief conversation with President Ronald Reagan, his eyes lit up when we talked about baseball and his radio career. It has often been said he might owe his reputation as the Great Communicator to baseball. During the Great Depression, Reagan launched his radio broadcasting career re-creating Chicago Cubs and White Sox games for a radio station in Des Moines, Iowa.

He later portrayed baseball players in the movies.

He was one of the first presidents to host Hall of Fame members in the State Dining Room in the White House. He started the practice before 1981's Opening Day.

During his off-the-cuff remarks, Reagan said: "The nostalgia is bubbling within me, and I may have to be dragged out of here because all of the stories that are coming up in my mind."

In 1952, the actor Reagan played pitching great Grover Cleveland Alexander in *The Winning Team.*

Bob Lemon would often talk about how during the filming of the movie he was Reagan's stand-in during scenes requiring a major league arm.

"I remember a part in the script that had Alexander hitting a catcher's mitt nailed to the side of a barn," Lemon once related during an induction weekend at the Hall of Fame.

"Piece of cake." He laughed and then said he hit everything but the catcher's mitt.

Lemon remembered Reagan asking, "Mind if I try?"

"One pitch, smack in the middle of that mitt," Lemon said. "I've never been so embarrassed in my life."

In the 2001 *Atlantic Monthly* story written by Carl M. Cannon, he related a wonderful yarn about Eisenhower:

"'When I was a small boy in Kansas,' Eisenhower once recalled, 'a friend of mine and I went fishing, and as we sat there in the warmth of a summer afternoon on a river bank, we talked about what we wanted to do when we grew up. I told him I wanted to be a real Major League Baseball player, a genuine professional like Honus Wagner. My friend said he'd like to be president of the United States. Neither of us got our wish!'"

In Cannon's piece, he also reveals an interesting story about Richard M. Nixon. (As an aside, I once interviewed Nixon at a Baltimore Colts football game at Memorial Stadium, where both the Colts and Orioles played then. All he wanted to talk about was baseball!) According to Cannon, shortly after the Watergate break-in that would envelop his administration, Nixon was at Camp David "writing down his all-time All-Star teams. Naturally, Nixon evaded the toughest decisions, putting together teams for different leagues and eras rather than coming up with a single list of players—thus avoiding, for example, having to choose from among Willie Mays, Joe DiMaggio, and Mickey Mantle for center field."

Even presidents who've had deep-seated passions for other sports have embraced baseball.

During an interview, Bill Clinton told me how his family was one of the first to have a television set in his hometown and he was able to watch St. Louis Cardinals games.

Clinton, as mentioned earlier, was at Shea Stadium on April 15, 1997, when Jackie Robinson's No. 42 was universally retired.

He was also on hand in Oriole Park at Camden Yards the night in 1995 when Cal Ripken Jr. surpassed Lou Gehrig's consecutive games record.

And he threw out the first pitch for the Orioles' opener in 1993.

He wore an orange-and-black Orioles warm-up jacket and admitted he practiced under the stands before the big moment.

The workout didn't help.

Clinton lobbed the ball high and wide.

Basketball is Barack Obama's favorite sport, but he has never tried to hide his love for the Chicago White Sox.

At the 2009 All-Star Game on July 14 at Busch Stadium in St. Louis, Obama wore a White Sox warm-up jacket when he went to the mound to throw out the first pitch. He lobbed the ball to the Cardinals' Albert Pujols, who had received the most votes for the All-Star Game and at that time was the toast of St. Louis.

Obama was accompanied on *Air Force One* to St. Louis by Hall of Famer Willie Mays, and during a visit with the All-Stars the president remarked, "I've got to say I'm getting old. All these ballplayers look really young to me."

Later, during an interview, he said: "This is our national pastime. It is such a reminder about what is great about this country. It's a real treat. This is as much fun as I've had in quite some time."

Memories of presidents and baseball for me remain so vivid— JFK, Nixon, Ford, Reagan, Carter, the Bushes, Clinton. As a journalist, I've been fortunate enough to tie the two together so often.

John F. Kennedy threw out four ceremonial first pitches during his time in office. I remember him at the 1962 All-Star Game in Washington and being on the field with many of the All-Stars. There was a photo in the *Washington Post* the next day showing JFK and Musial embracing.

At the time, Kennedy was 45 and Musial 41.

Later, Musial recalled a conversation with the president.

Musial remembered saying to Kennedy: "They say you're too young to be president and I'm too old to be playing baseball, but we're both here."

Musial and the National League won that game 3–1. Musial batted .330 in 1962.

No moment, however, has been such a lasting memory, or meaningful, as that night at Yankee Stadium—October 30, 2001.

Baseball and the president were so important—an exemplary moment when the two joined hands to help our deeply wounded country try to heal.

"I went to the batting cage to loosen up my arm," Bush said. "A Secret Service agent strapped a bulletproof vest to my chest. After a few warm-up pitches, the great Yankees shortstop Derek Jeter dropped in to take some swings.

"We talked a little. Then, he asked, 'Hey, Mr. President, are you going to throw from the mound or from in front of it?'

"I asked what he thought. 'Throw from the mound,' Jeter said, 'or else they'll boo you.' I agreed to do it. On his way out, he looked over his shoulder and said, 'But don't bounce it. They'll boo you.'"

In *Decision Points*, Bush added: "Nine months into the presidency, I was used to being introduced to a crowd. But I'd never had a feeling like I did when Bob Sheppard, the Yankees legendary public address announcer, belted out. 'Please welcome the president of the United States.'

"I climbed to the mound, gave a wave and a thumbs-up, and peered in at the catcher, Todd Greene. He looked a lot farther away than sixty feet, six inches. My adrenaline was surging. The ball felt like a shot put. I would up and let it fly.

"The noise in the stadium was like a sonic boom. 'USA, USA, USA!'"

The president threw a strike.

13

Take Me Out
to the Ball Game

America was without baseball much of the summer of 1981. The players had gone on strike June 12 and fans were suffering; they were enduring the sport's first major strike and needed a baseball fix.

The players didn't return to the field until the All-Star Game in Cleveland on August 9, but fans' spirits were lifted when singer-composer Terry Cashman gave them an infectious melody filled with pure nostalgia for simpler times and a clear love for baseball.

Cashman's 1981 hit "Talkin' Baseball, Willie, Mickey, and the Duke," celebrated the golden era of baseball in general, and center fielders in particular.

Ah, yes.

Hum the melody and if you love and have a passion for baseball there'll be a rush of adrenaline.

Talkin' baseball…
Willie, Mickey, and the Duke. (Say hey, say hey, say hey)
It was Willie, Mickey, and the Duke (Say hey, say hey, say hey)
I'm talkin' Willie, Mickey, and the Duke (Say hey, say hey, say hey)

Willie, Mickey, and the Duke. (Say hey, say hey, say hey)
Say Willie, Mickey, and the Duke. (Say hey, say hey, say hey)

Music and baseball. So important.

Just as much a part of our national pastime as the movies.

They go hand-in-hand.

On August 5, 2001, Bill Mazeroski, whose dramatic walk-off home run at Forbes Field gave Pittsburgh a thrilling 1960 World Series championship over the favored Yankees, was finally inducted into the Hall of Fame. Maz walked to the podium that Sunday afternoon, with thousands watching, said a few words, and broke down. Tears flowed as he retreated to his seat. He received a standing ovation from the Cooperstown, New York, throng.

I wrote that day: "Tom Hanks had it wrong. There *is* crying in baseball."

Was there a better way to describe Mazeroski's failure to deliver his acceptance speech?

The day before, Maz told me: "I never thought I'd be here for an occasion such as this, me getting inducted. It's something I never counted on…. It's going to be interesting tomorrow—if I can get my speech out."

And he didn't.

Had it not been for the excellent 1992 movie *A League of Their Own*, with Hanks, Geena Davis, Rosie O'Donnell, Madonna, et al, Mazeroski's emotional breakdown wouldn't have had the perfect tie-in. Or the lasting impact.

Movies have a way of doing that.

The memorable line "There's no crying in baseball" lives on from the movie directed by Penny Marshall that featured Tom Hanks as a washed-up major leaguer, which some say is based on real-life Hall of Famers Jimmie Foxx and Hack Wilson.

Hanks was the manager of a women's baseball team created during World War II at a time when scores of major leaguers went off to defend our country.

A League of Their Own fittingly concludes at the Hall of Fame in Cooperstown as the players, with emotions flowing, come

together to be honored one last time. Many of the real women who were the reason for the film are pictured at the end.

Yes, there *is* crying in baseball.

In Bill Madden's 2003 book *Pride of October*, Yogi Berra remembers, "Afterward [Mazeroski's homer] Mickey [Mantle] cried, and that was the only time I can remember not being able to bring myself to go over to the other clubhouse and congratulate 'em."

173

Great lines from baseball movies endure.

How many times have you heard, or yourself repeated, "If you build it, he will come." That comes from the excellent 1989 picture *Field of Dreams.*

Or "Candlesticks always make a nice gift," from 1988's *Bull Durham.*

And, of course, "There's no crying in baseball."

Famed documentary director Peter Miller says: "Baseball and film are married in ways that I think reflect so much about the American character and about American culture…. Baseball emerges in America as the central cultural iconic institution that unites us all, then film comes along a little bit later and does the same thing."

According to Hall of Fame historian Bill Francis, an authority on baseball movies, the sport has been represented on film dating to the late 19th century, starting with the Thomas Edison–produced *The Ball Game* in 1898.

Right off the Bat, a five-reel comedy drama released in 1915, is generally regarded as the first feature-length baseball movie.

A biopic on the life of former outfielder "Turkey" Mike Donlin, who left the game in 1914 after 12 big-league seasons, not only featured Donlin playing himself but Hall of Fame manager John McGraw also made an appearance.

After *Right Off the Bat* was released, *The New York Times* wrote: "For the first time baseball has been put on the screen in such a fashion that even an Englishman can understand it—and that is accomplishing the impossible."

A short and certainly not complete list of some of the more popular or critically acclaimed baseball movie titles over the years, which count farce, dramas, romantic comedies, biographies, and even musicals among them, include: *The Pride of the Yankees* (1942), *The Babe Ruth Story* (1948), *The Stratton Story* (1949), *The Jackie Robinson Story* (1950), *Angels in the Outfield* (1951), *Fear Strikes Out* (1957), *Damn Yankees* (1958), *Bang the Drum Slowly* (1973), *The Bad News Bears* (1976), *The Bingo Long Traveling All-Stars and Motor Kings* (1976), *The Natural* (1984), *Bull Durham* (1988), *Eight*

Men Out (1988), *Field of Dreams* (1989), *Major League* (1989), *A League of Their Own* (1992), *The Sandlot* (1993), *Cobb* (1994), *For Love of the Game* (1999), *61** (2001), *The Rookie* (2002), *Sugar* (2009), *Moneyball* (2011), and *Trouble with the Curve* (2012).

And in the spring of 2013, the highly acclaimed *42: The Jackie Robinson Story* was released. Chadwick Boseman played the role of Robinson as he broke baseball's color barrier in 1947. Harrison Ford was Branch Rickey, the Dodgers general manager who made the decision to change the face of major league baseball.

Kevin Costner, who starred in a trio of baseball movies—*Bull Durham*, *Field of Dreams*, and *For Love of the Game*—says you can't make a baseball movie about baseball.

"I think it always has to be about people," Costner said. "And what you need to do is honor the athleticism it requires to make such a movie, because even non-athletes can tell what an unathletic movement looks like."

In some sense the baseball movie has defined the way Americans view the game and their relationship to it.

Actor James Earl Jones has appeared in *Field of Dreams*, *The Bingo Long Traveling All-Stars and Motor Kings*, and *The Sandlot*. But during an appearance at the Hall of Fame for a 15th anniversary celebration of *Field of Dreams* in 2004, he was asked why he thinks *Field of Dreams* remains as popular as when it was first released.

"Because it's not really about baseball. It's really about other things," Jones said. "It's about fathers and sons. The mom is the first companion, the second companion is pop. Pop doesn't become important until one day he says let's got out in the backyard and play catch. That's when the bonding starts in most families; at least it's a poetic way of looking at it. That's kind of America."

When I was a youngster growing up in a tiny Delaware town, there were several vacant lots next to our house.

Baseball was my passion, but I thought if I built a baseball diamond on the overgrown lots my friends would come to play the game. I was convinced "if I built it, they would come." Unlike Ray Kinsella, the Iowa farmer Kevin Costner played in *Field of Dreams*, I can't remember hearing any voice but my own.

I do know that when I saw the movie I thought back to my childhood and how I drove my parents crazy using my dad's lawn mower and garden tractor to build my own *Field of Dreams*.

Of course, after Ray hears the voice—despite the financial foolishness of such an act—he cuts down part of his corn crop and creates a baseball field. And then one night Shoeless Joe Jackson, the disgraced face of the Chicago Black Sox gambling scandal, walks out from a row of the tall cornstalks to play on the baseball diamond.

From that evolves a touching, moving story about forgiveness, regrets, and broken dreams.

It's really about chasing dreams and the deepest love of baseball.

For me, it's one of the most treasured movies ever produced, because from the youngest age I was certain if I built it, they would come. And they did.

Seldom has a baseball movie been as interwoven with the actual philosophy and strategy of the game currently on display throughout the major leagues as it is in *Moneyball*.

Based on the Michael Lewis best-selling 2003 book, *Moneyball* depicts how Oakland general manager Billy Beane (played by Brad Pitt) ignored the traditional ways of scouting players to build a major league team.

His theories, based on analytical studies, have been talked about—and used—throughout the major leagues. As an aside, his Oakland Athletics have won six American League Western Division titles the past 16 years and have won 90 or more games eight of the last 14 seasons.

Former player Billy Sample wrote, produced, co-directed, and starred in a baseball movie called *Reunion 108*.

"I wrote a screenplay and submitted it to the Hoboken Film Festival, where I got to talk to veteran actor Robert Loggia about his baseball-playing days," says Sample. "The screenplay took top honors."

It was released in October 2013.

According to Tim Wiles, the Hall of Fame's former director of research, "Take Me Out to the Ball Game" is the third-most frequently played song in American culture after "Happy Birthday" and "The Star-Spangled Banner."

Without a doubt, it's baseball's anthem.

There was no better place to hear it or sing it than at Wrigley Field when Harry Caray was alive.

"All right, let me hear you, good and loud," Harry, mic in hand and leaning out of the broadcast booth, would shout to the fans.

"A one, a two, a three!"
Take me out to the ball game,
Take me out with the crowd.
Buy me some peanuts and cracker jack,
I don't care if I never get back,
Let me root, root, root for the home team (Cubbies),
If they don't win it's a shame.
For it's one, two, three strikes, you're out,
At the old ball game."

Former pitcher Larry Andersen, a friend who's now a Phillies' broadcaster, has a humorous knack for putting things in perspective. Especially when it comes to "Take Me Out to the Ball Game."

"In the seventh inning fans all get up and sing, 'Take Me Out to the Ball Game,' and they're already there!" Andersen says. "It's really a stupid thing to say and I don't know who made 'em sing it. Why would somebody that's there get up and sing 'Take me out to the ball game?' The first person to do it must have been a moron."

It could have been the beloved maverick Bill Veeck, and he was no moron.

The song was written in 1908 by Jack Norworth and Albert Von Tilzer, Tin Pan Alley songwriters, and, according to research by Wiles, the first known time it was performed in a ballpark was 1934.

Says Wiles: "The story goes that Norworth penned the lyrics one day while riding one of Manhattan's new subway trains north toward the Polo Grounds. He remembered seeing a sign advertising that day's game and pulling out a pencil and paper to scribble down a set of lyrics, which Von Tilzer would later pair with a tune he had composed."

Give Veeck credit for realizing the impact the legendary broadcaster Harry Caray would ultimately have sticking his head out of the both and leading fans in singing the song.

"I tried it in Milwaukee, Cleveland, St. Louis, and Chicago the first time, but it never worked," the late Veeck said. "Finally, I got the right guy. It does a lot for the game and gets the fans involved even if the White Sox are losing."

Caray, states *Baseball Almanac*, is credited with singing "Take Me Out to the Ball Game" first at a ball game in 1971. He said he'd always sing it, "because I think it's the only song I knew the words to!"

Harry, who later moved to the Cubs, was broadcasting White Sox games in 1976. On Opening Day, Veeck noticed the fans were singing along with Caray, so a secret microphone was placed in the broadcast booth the following day to allow all the fans to hear him.

"Harry, anybody in the ballpark hearing you sing knows that he can sing as well as you can. Probably better than you can," Veeck teased. "So, he or she sings along. Hell, if you had a good singing voice you'd intimidate them, and nobody would join in."

Originally, Caray didn't like the idea, but it later became his signature, especially after moving to the Cubs and Wrigley Field in 1982.

Because the Cubs were seen nationally on WGN, the song became even more popular. Caray died in 1998, but the Cubs have continued the tradition with celebrities leading fans.

According to ASCAP data, "Take Me Out to the Ball Game" has been recorded by over 500 artists and has been used in television and the movies over 1,200 times.

Terry Cashman is the legitimate "Balladeer of Baseball."

Born Dennis Minogue, Cashman himself was a minor league right-handed pitcher in the Detroit Tigers organization. He never made it on the field, but changed his tune and has been honored by the Hall of Fame for his musical contributions to baseball.

During an interview for this book, Cashman told me he was inspired to write "Talkin' Baseball" while attending an Old-Timers' Day at Shea Stadium.

Willie Mays, Mickey Mantle, Duke Snider, and Joe DiMaggio were photographed walking in from center field in their uniforms.

"Somebody took a picture from behind in which you see them walking together toward home plate from center field," Cashman said from his Bronx, New York, apartment. "You see their numbers—24, 7, 4, and 5. I thought this picture was incredible because of what it represented in the terms of baseball history in New York City in the 1940s and 1950s.

"When we released the record, we wanted to use that picture. We had gotten in touch with Mantle, Mays, and Snider's representatives. We said we'd give them some money; they were all very happy and agreed. We tried and tried, but couldn't reach DiMaggio.

"In the meantime we have these records coming out. We wanted to use the picture on the sleeve, never reached DiMaggio, so we airbrushed him out of the photo because we couldn't reach Joe."

The next year, on July 19, 1982, at the Cracker Jack Old-Timers Classic at Washington's RFK Stadium—the night 75-year-old Luke Appling homered off 61-year-old Warren Spahn—Cashman was invited to sing "Talkin' Baseball."

"The night before the game there was a cocktail party," said Cashman. "I knew Richie Ashburn, Ralph Kiner, and some of the others. I'm schmoozing with these guys and Kiner says, 'There's Joe DiMaggio. You want to meet him?' I walk over and Kiner says, 'This is the guy who wrote the new baseball song.' DiMaggio stares at me and says, 'You're the one who took me out of the picture.' I said, 'Joe we tried every way in the world to get up with you. We couldn't use the picture without your permission.' He said, 'Oh, I've had songs written about me.'

"It was an uncomfortable situation for everyone. To get out of the situation, I said, 'Joe, don't worry. I have another idea and I think you'll like it.'"

Later that year, at the Hall of Fame during the inductions for Hank Aaron and Frank Robinson, Cashman was invited to sing "Talkin' Baseball," plus a new song he'd just written called "Cooperstown, the Town Where Baseball Lives."

"In that song, the lyrics say 'I'm going to the place where baseball lives—Ruth and Cobb and Joe DiMaggio. Sunny days and Willie Mays….'

"I finish the song, get a tremendous ovation and walk to the back of the stage and there's DiMaggio. He has a big smile on his face and shakes my hand. He says, 'Now, I know what you meant in Washington with an idea I'd like.' The hell with Mickey, Willie, and the Duke. He's with Cobb and Ruth. After that, he was always very nice to me."

Actually, Terry said when he was writing "Talkin' Baseball," "I kept trying to fit Joe DiMaggio into the lyrics and it wasn't working."

Without Joe D., he said, the verse flowed rather easily.

"I sat down and wrote the whole thing in 20 minutes," he added. "It's really all about three center fielders, all of whom played in the same city at the same time and they're all in the Hall of Fame."

Soon after Cashman released "Talkin' Baseball" in 1981, he was invited by the Seattle Mariners to sing the national anthem and his new song at Opening Day for the second half of the season (following the strike).

"They asked me to go out there because, as their manager Rene Lachemann said, 'You're the only good thing that's happened in baseball this year. They're sending you out there [to sing] because they hate the owners and they hate the players,'" Cashman said.

From that moment other teams began asking him to adapt "Talkin' Baseball" with new lyrics for their teams.

After over two years, he'd done every major league team.

And it's become one of the greatest songs written for baseball:

The Whiz Kids had won it,
Bobby Thomson had done it,
And Yogi read the comics all the while.
Rock 'n' roll was being born,
Marijuana, we would scorn,
So down on the corner,
The national past-time went on trial.

We're talkin' baseball!
Kluszewski, Campanella.
Talkin' baseball!
The Man and Bobby Feller.
The Scooter, the Barber, and the Newk,
They knew 'em all from Boston to Dubuque.
Especially Willie, Mickey, and the Duke.

Well, Casey was winning,
Hank Aaron was beginning,
One Robby going out, one coming in.
Kiner and Midget Gaedel,
The Thumper and Mel Parnell,
And Ike was the only one winning down in Washington.

We're talkin' baseball!
Kluszewski, Campanella.
Talkin' baseball!
The Man and Bobby Feller.
The Scooter, the Barber, and the Newk,
They knew 'em all from Boston to Dubuque.
Especially Willie, Mickey, and the Duke.

Now my old friend, The Bachelor,
Well, he swore he was the Oklahoma Kid.
And Cookie played hooky,
To go and see the Duke.
And me, I always loved Willie Mays,
Those were the days!

Well, now it's the '80s,
And Brett is the greatest,
And Bobby Bonds can play for everyone.
Rose is at the Vet,
And Rusty again is a Met,
And the great Alexander is pitchin' again in Washington.

I'm talkin' baseball!
Like Reggie, Quisenberry.
Talkin' baseball!
Carew and Gaylord Perry,
Seaver, Garvey, Schmidt, and Vida Blue,
If Cooperstown is calling, it's no fluke.
They'll be with Willie, Mickey, and the Duke.

Willie, Mickey, and the Duke. (Say hey, say hey, say hey)
It was Willie, Mickey, and the Duke (Say hey, say hey, say hey)
I'm talkin' Willie, Mickey, and the Duke (Say hey, say hey, say hey)
Willie, Mickey, and the Duke. (Say hey, say hey, say hey)
Say Willie, Mickey, and the Duke. (Say hey, say hey, say hey).

When Cashman was growing up in New York City he and his friends would go to the street corner and wait for deliveries of the first edition of the *Daily News* and *Mirror* "and we'd be talking baseball. We'd be arguing about who was better, Williams or DiMaggio, Musial or Williams. There were all these arguments, but the main one was Willie, Mickey, and the Duke. Who was the best center fielder?

"That's where I got the idea. You know, I say 'down on the corner the national pastime went on trial.' Then, I use Kluszewski and Campanella and all the names from the 1950s."

In 1996, Cashman wrote "The Ballad of Herb Score," which he calls one of his most personal and heartfelt efforts. He wrote that after meeting Score at the restaurant of former big-league slugger Rusty Staub.

"Bet you never heard of Herbie Score, but after the winter of '54, the Indian signals said send us a kid with smoke," Cashman's lyrics go. *"He blew 'em away in '55, this redhead southpaw, man alive, bet you never heard of Herbie Score."*

Score, of course, struck out 245 batters as a 22-year-old in 1955. He won 16 games that season and 20 in 1956, but on May 7, 1957, was struck in the face by a line drive off the bat of the Yankees' Gil McDougald and could never pitch as well as he did the first two seasons.

"The gods of the diamond change like the weather," the ballad goes. *"They give us a natural, then they take him forever. And that's what they did to Herbie Score.*

"The gods of the diamond, they play a strange game. They give us a light, then they blow out the flame. And that's what they did to Herbie Score."

Score, who died on November 11, 2008, won just 17 games during the five seasons after he was hit.

Cashman is convinced "The Ballad of Herb Score" keeps the memory alive of a man Terry believes could have been one of the game's greatest pitchers.

Music has a way of doing that.

"I think baseball has such a rich history," Cashman said. "It's part of the fabric of America. Even if you're not a baseball fan, even if you're not American, you know what a home run is, you know what a third-base coach is, and you know who Babe Ruth was. It's part of our culture.

"And for me, it has a personal place in my heart. My father loved baseball, my mother loved it and my older brothers loved it. Next to family and religion, it's something that's very, very important to people."

Baseball will always have music and cherish it.

In many modern ballparks today, each time a hitter strolls to the plate or a pitcher warms up, he is accompanied by a personally selected theme song. While many of us fans have noticed this trend, few have thought of its deeper implications for popular culture.

Nothing defines a culture at the popular level better than its music, something which almost everyone enjoys—try to find someone who doesn't like music on at least some level. Another great indicator of a society's cultural values and passions is its sports.

Writes research guru Tim Wiles: "Surveying the thick file of clippings labeled 'music' at the Hall of Fame Library…there are so many connections between baseball and music, it's safe to say there are two national pastimes!"

The first two baseball songs, "The Baseball Polka" and "Baseball Days," were written in 1858. The first ballpark organ was installed at Wrigley Field in 1941. Just five years later, the National League felt it necessary to ban the song "Three Blind Mice," after the organist at Ebbets Field made a habit of playing it after close calls which went against the Dodgers. The Brooklyn Sym-Phony was an inspired group of fans who serenaded the Ebbets Field crowd, without the benefit of formal musical training.

The Yankees have even inspired a Broadway musical, *Damn Yankees*, about the team that's so hard to beat, one's thoughts turn to desperate measures. There have been several teams with theme songs—the 1979 Pirates bonded over Sister Sledge's "We Are Family." The Yanks of 1940 liked to "Roll Out the Barrel," and of course the 2004 Red Sox breathed new life into an old Royal Rooters classic, "Tessie," as performed by the Dropkick Murphys.

"Where have you gone, Joe DiMaggio?" asked Paul Simon poignantly in the song "Mrs. Robinson," and the great center fielder was also the subject of two songs: "Joltin' Joe DiMaggio," by Les Brown and His Band of Renown, and "Joe DiMaggio Done It Again," by Woody Guthrie.

Irving Berlin's 1926 composition, "Along Came Ruth," was one of nearly a dozen songs inspired by the Babe's home run prowess. The late Ernie Harwell penned a 1974 tribute to Babe and his successor Hank Aaron, titled "Move Over Babe, Here Comes Henry."

One of the finest of all baseball songs is "Did You See Jackie Robinson Hit that Ball?" by Count Basie and His Orchestra.

Music and the movies?

Baseball is steeped with a rich history, built around great players and their achievements.

Nothing complements the sport more than music and motion pictures.

After all, we're talkin' baseball, and that is the bottom line.

14

The American Dream
(Cuban Edition)

Tony Oliva says he's blessed.

"I have been so lucky," he said. "At every stop along the way I've been lucky and I'm very thankful. This has been a dream. I believe God had a big plan for me."

When I told Tony this book was about baseball and America, he interrupted with "and about the dream. Dreams are important. Put that in there."

Agreed.

Yes, this is symbolic of the American experience, part of which is usually that initial immigration, treacherous and lonely, which many of our grandfathers and great-grandfathers (and mothers) did, and which the Cuban players still have to do today.

During the 10 years I spoke at MLB's Rookie Career Development Program, it became obvious how young players from the Dominican Republic and Venezuela and others who left their families and homes were intimidated being in a foreign country, struggling with our language and our customs.

But, like Tony Oliva, they were chasing the small chance of making it in Major League Baseball.

The same was true, although not as evident, for the players coming from Japan. The globalization of baseball has mirrored the globalization of business and society as a whole.

Tony Oliva is important because he has come from being a dirt-poor farmer near Havana to an American baseball icon, popular throughout the game and even more so because of his roots in the Midwest.

It wasn't easy. He had to put up with loneliness, being broke, not speaking English, and living in a segregated society with "colored" restaurants and poor rooming situations.

"But I've been very lucky," he interrupted. "Lucky at every stop."

Tony Oliva should be in the Hall of Fame, but that's another story for another day.

Tony is now 75.

He played only for the Minnesota Twins, but during his 15 years was one of Major League Baseball's premier players.

Three times he was the American League batting champion, eight consecutive years he was an All-Star, he won a Gold Glove in 1966, and I almost forgot—he was the AL's Rookie of the Year in 1964, only three years after Twins officials proclaimed, "He'll never hit in the major leagues."

"I think about that today and have to laugh," said Oliva, modestly pointing out for "five of my first seven years I led the American League in hits."

Tony Oliva was special because he had explosive power to go with his remarkable hit-to-all-fields swing.

It was a long way from Pinar del Rio, Cuba.

What makes Tony's story so intriguing is that in the winter of 1961 he was one of 22 Cuban baseball prospects who flew to Mexico, then on to Florida to attend a tryout camp and chase their dreams.

Eleven were signed and 11 didn't make it. Pedro Oliva Jr. got a pink slip.

According to Bob Fowler, who wrote the 1973 book *Tony O! The Trials and Triumphs of Tony Oliva,* Tony used the name of his older brother and his passport to enter the United States.

When Oliva keeps saying how lucky he was, he quickly adds that he was one of the last players to leave Cuba before Fidel Castro put a halt to immigration. The Castro revolution had begun in 1959.

"I was very lucky to get out of Cuba when I did in 1961," he said. "Two weeks later they had the Bay of Pigs invasion. If I had still been in Cuba, I wouldn't have been able to leave. I was in Mexico with the other guys when that happened.

"Then all 22 of us from Cuba went to the tryout camp with the Minnesota Twins at Fernandina Beach, Florida. They cut 11 of us and I was one of them. I was so disappointed and didn't know what to do. I couldn't sleep—or eat.

"So, I then went to Charlotte to wait there before I went back home. But I was unable to go back home, so I stayed and finally got my big chance. I was lucky because I became a big prospect."

But before that, he says he was not only depressed, disappointed, and heartbroken to have his dream smashed at the tryout camp, but he was stranded in a foreign country.

"I had no place to go but home then," he said. "I really didn't want to go back to Cuba because I wanted to be a ballplayer. It was my dream. I cannot tell you how sad I was."

While others disagreed, Phil Howser, general manager of Minnesota's Double-A franchise in Charlotte thought Oliva had potential. He invited him to work with the Charlotte Hornets.

Each day Tony would report to the ballpark and work out for hours.

"I'd catch fly balls and take batting practice as much as I could," he said. "I was even there alone when the Hornets were on the road. I worked and worked and worked. *Hard.*

"It was very lonely for me. I missed my family, couldn't speak English, and there was no one to talk to.

"I thought of my parents and brothers back on the farm in Cuba and I missed them. A couple of times I almost left to go home, but there was the revolution going on and I truthfully had no way to get there."

He also told Fowler: "I had to walk to the ballpark each day. It was four miles. I got only $3 a day expense money. I couldn't take a cab, or I wouldn't have money to eat. I couldn't take a bus because I couldn't speak English.

"Phil Howser wrote down on a slip of paper things for me to eat. One slip said 'ham and eggs' and another said 'fried chicken.' All I had to do was hand one slip to the waitress.

"I ate ham and eggs and fried chicken for three months. It got so I hated it."

Pausing, in our conversation, Oliva repeated, "I was so lucky."

Charlie Manuel, who grew up in the Twins' organization as a player, and later became one of the game's top managers in Cleveland and Philadelphia, said Oliva had a really tough time in the beginning, but because he was so determined he made it work.

"He was ahead of me in the minors and got to the big leagues in a hurry," said Manuel. "Minnie Mendoza, a guy I played with in the minors, was also from Cuba. He let Oliva stay with him in Charlotte rather than go back to Cuba. Phil Howser was a good judge of talent.

"They waited until the rookie season opened and Howser, also a friend of mine, let Tony play for Wytheville. When Tony first signed, he wasn't a good fielder, but had a great arm. He could always hit and worked hard on his fielding."

Because of Howser's faith and Oliva's hard work and determination he improved greatly—so much so he was assigned to that Class A team at Wytheville of the Appalachian League. He hit .410 and his career was on its way. He was named Appalachian League Rookie of the Year and promoted to Charlotte for 1962. After batting .350, on September 9 he made his major league debut with the Twins and played in nine games.

Most of 1963 was spent at Dallas–Fort Worth of the Pacific Coast League, where he hit .304. He played seven games with the Twins in September and began his rise to stardom in 1964.

Oliva says, "I always tell people if I had been a good fielder, I would have made it to the major leagues out of rookie ball. I was able to hit and run and throw, but I had to work very hard on my fielding.

"I am very proud of that Gold Glove because I wanted to become a good fielder like Al Kaline. I patterned my fielding after him. I wanted to be like him. And three years after I made it to the major leagues in 1964, I won a Gold Glove."

Manuel is convinced that "by the time he got to the big leagues he was an above-average fielder, good speed, accurate throwing arm—yes, a good right fielder."

As a three-time batting champ, I believe Oliva was destined for the Hall of Fame on the baseball writers' ballot until he suffered a serious knee injury in 1971.

He appeared in just 10 games the next year, then put in four seasons as the designated hitter before retiring in 1976, at the age of 36, with his .304 career average and 1,917 hits.

Overall, he's had four knee operations.

"I think if he'd been able to play longer, no question he would've made the Hall of Fame," said Manuel. "The fact he played only 15 years hurt his chances, but I still think he belongs."

Because Oliva didn't receive the required 75 percent of the votes any of his 15 years on the Baseball Writers Association of

America ballot, his only chance now is to be elected by the Veterans Committee.

For most of the 1970s Oliva was hampered by the knee, leg, and shoulder injuries.

Rod Carew, his roommate, said he often heard Tony "moaning and groaning" and getting up to obtain ice for his sore knees during the night.

Oliva missed 34 games in 1968, but rebounded the next two years with .309, 24 homers, 101 runs batted in, and .325, 23, 107, respectively.

He missed all but 10 games of the 1972 season, which required season-ending surgery. After that, he became the Twins' DH.

In 1981, Larry Ritter and Donald Honig included Oliva in their book *The 100 Greatest Baseball Players of All Time.*

They explained what they called "the Smoky Joe Wood Syndrome," in which a player of truly exceptional talent but whose career was curtailed by injury, in spite of not having had career statistics that would quantitatively rank him with the all-time greats, should still be included on their list of the 100 greatest players.

Bill James determined that Oliva was a "viable Hall of Fame candidate," but ultimately didn't endorse him as a Hall of Famer.

However, several contemporaries have endorsed him, including fellow Cuban Tony Perez, who mentioned him in his 2000 Cooperstown induction speech, saying he hoped that Oliva would soon be in the Hall of Fame.

"Charlie blamed me all the time," Oliva said of Manuel. "Charlie said, 'Because of you I'm not playing in the big leagues.' He was also a right fielder. I joked with him that every year I had to hold out to get my little raise. I told him there was always an opening for him."

Manuel was mostly a bench player, filling in at times for Bob Allison and Oliva.

"He kept me on the bench," said Manuel. "We had two of the best corner guys in baseball. We had myself, Graig Nettles—all these left-handed hitters—and we were young. They didn't have a platoon system back in those days. Billy Martin was the manager and would give Allison a rest. That's when Nettles and I got to play. Nettles would play third base and Harmon Killebrew would play first.

"I loved Tony Oliva. I always pulled for him."

Manuel and Oliva were teammates only four years (1969–1972), but Charlie says "for the short time I was with him he was as good as any hitter in the majors. That was also kind of a dead-ball era. Home runs were really down. The most he ever hit was 32, and that was in his rookie year. He was a tremendous hitter, unreal.

"When Catfish Hunter was pitching for Oakland, Tony would wear him out. I remember one day he hit two home runs off Catfish about as far as you could ever hit the ball. He came back to the dugout and said, 'I hit that ball pretty good.' He looked at me and asked, 'What's his name?' He didn't even know who Catfish was."

Oliva says when he got to the United States there were a lot of good players in Cuba and Latin America, but it was hard for them to break in. There just wasn't a good system for them.

"I was lucky. I went boom-boom, and to the major leagues in 1964."

Tony loves to talk about his wife.

He started dating Gordette Du Bois, who was from Hitchcock, South Dakota, in the mid-1960s. They were married in 1968 and settled in Bloomington, Minnesota.

They still live in the house he bought in 1972. And his four children, with the exception of one, live within 10 miles of their parents. They have four grandchildren.

Tony jokes that his favorite meal is no longer ham and eggs, or fried chicken.

"It's now steak," he said. "Because I can afford it; I've been known to eat it three times a day.

"It's nice having a family," he said. "It was always great to come home to them after a game or a road trip."

Fowler said when Oliva was playing, he often would be in gift shops, buying toys and clothes for his wife and children.

During our long conversation, Oliva says he enjoys returning to Cuba "about once a year to visit friends and family. My brother Juan Carlos played for the Cuban national team for many years. Now he is the pitching coach for the Pinar del Rio's club."

He said when he came to the United States in 1961 most of the foreign players in the major leagues and minor leagues were Cuban players.

"After 1961, it was hard for Cuban players to come here. There was always a lot of talent there because baseball is so popular. All the young boys played it."

During Spring Training in 1999, the Orioles went to Cuba for an historic exhibition.

Tony Oliva was invited by Major League Baseball to join the U.S. contingent for the one game, but declined.

"I didn't want to go over for one day," he said. "I have a lot of family in Cuba. If I go to Cuba, I'm going to go to visit my family.

"If the Minnesota Twins club goes and invites me, I'll go. But if it's somebody else, I don't think it makes any sense for me to go just for one day.

"That's why I didn't make the trip."

Was it politics?

"Some people don't go for political reasons, but I think political reasons are different," he said. "Sports is one thing, politics is another. This was just about a baseball game. Nothing more.

"I know it's hard for a lot of people to understand that. A lot of people have mixed feelings about it."

Oliva said he wanted to make sure when people talked about that 1999 groundbreaking exhibition they put it in proper perspective.

Oliva has always supported Commissioner Bud Selig. He said when the 1999 game was proposed, "I believe that if the commissioner of baseball thinks for one moment that this game we play in Cuba would hurt baseball, then he would not allow it to happen.

"When I look back, the game was good for everybody. I think it's good for the people who play the game, I think it's good for the fans, and I think it's good for the people who work in this business.

"After we die, baseball is still going to be here. It's still going to be strong."

In 1973, Oliva did return to Cuba for a month. It was his first trip back since fateful 1961, when he left to attend the Twins' tryout camp in Florida—and told his large family he'd be back in six months.

"It was a wonderful trip," he told reporter Bob Fowler. "I saw all my brothers and sisters, my mother and father, and other relatives.

During the 1960s, '70s, and even into the early '80s, Oliva believes Cuba probably had the best amateur baseball talent.

Or as Peter C. Bjarkman wrote in *The National Pastime*: "The ballparks in Havana, Holguin, Mantanzas, and other cities were home to some of the greatest diamond stars that United States fans never saw.

"Heroes of this era included Wilfredo 'El Hombre Hit' Sanchez, Antonio Munoz, Manuel Alacron, Augustin Marquetti, and Braudilio Vinent.

"Lefty-swinging Wil Sanchez was one of the greatest hitters in Cuban history, winning no fewer than five batting titles, including the first back-to-back pair in 1969 and 1970. His lifetime mark of .332 trails only those of Linares (.373), the league's first-ever .400 hitter, and Alexander Ramos (.337), who reached the 1,000-hit plateau."

Cuba's rich baseball history stretches back long before Castro and the 1959 revolution. The game was first played on the island two years before the birth of the National League.

Cuban Enrique Esteban Bellan became the first-ever Latin big leaguer when he appeared with the National Association Troy Haymakers in 1871.

Cubans also appeared in the National League before World War I. Armando Marsans and Rafael Almeida played for the Cincinnati Reds in 1911. And Adolfo Luque was a legitimate star when he won 27 games for the Reds in 1923 after originally playing for the Boston Braves in 1914—long before baseball integrated in 1947.

Bjarkman points out, "It was the post–World War II period that saw a full-scale Cuban invasion of the major leagues—first with a handful of Washington Senators journeymen, then with flashy 1950s stars like Minnie Minoso, Tony Taylor, Camilo Pascual, and Pete Ramos, and finally with Zoilo Versailles, Luis Tiant, and Tony Perez, who made their marks in the 1960s and 1970s."

And, of course, Tony Oliva.

"Back home in Havana," Bjarkman writes, "the Cubans had been hosting top-flight Winter League play between black and white Cubans and North Americans since the mid-1920s. They were also dominating the world amateur scene throughout the 1930s and 1940s, and the Winter Professional Caribbean World Series during its first phase from 1949 through 1960. Cuba won the first title in Havana in 1949 and seven of the first dozen competitions.

"A top pro league in the '40s and '50s featured legendary teams representing Club Havana, Almendares, Cienfuegos, and Marianao, and showcased a mixture of Cuban stars and major leaguers in sparkling new El Cerro Stadium. Now, it's revamped and renamed Estadio Latinoamericano."

Oliva, sadness in his voice, said most of this changed, or ended, with Castro's takeover.

Prior to Castro, the majority of foreign players in major league baseball were from Cuba.

"Now, it's the Dominican Republic and Venezuela," said Oliva.

The 2013 Opening Day rosters of all major league teams featured 214 players born outside the United States. That's a percentage of 28.2, fourth highest of all-time. The Dominican Republic topped the list with 89 players, followed by Venezuela with 63.

Cuba ranked fourth overall with just 15 players, but surpassed its 2002 total of 11 and 2011 (12) for its highest total since at least 1995. Interesting is the fact the Milwaukee Brewers have the most foreign-born players with a total of 14 on a roster that spans a major league-high seven different countries and territories.

"Puerto Rico is also important," said Oliva. "Thirteen major leaguers came from there last season."

Because immigration to the U.S. is still banned for Cuban players, we've all heard the horror stories about scary boat trips and other episodes as to how they have made it to the major leagues.

Jose Contreras, Livan Hernandez, Orlando "El Duque" Hernandez, Danys Baez, Brayan Pena, and Alex Sanchez are just a sampling of Cubans who've made their way to the major leagues since Castro came in to power.

Omar Minaya, former Expos and Mets general manager, has always paid close attention to players coming out of Cuba.

"What distinguishes the Cubans from other Latin players is their ability to turn it up a notch," he said. "They are able to be very relaxed and at the same time play with power and speed.

"They play the game with a lot more flair, more so than the Dominicans. But they have a power game that other Latin American countries don't have."

Cuba finished second to Japan in the first World Baseball Classic in 2006, was sixth in 2009, and fifth in 2013. Overall in the WBC, Cuba has a 13–7 record, which places it fourth among all the countries.

Cuban defector "El Duque" Hernandez, who made headlines when he was signed and pitched for the Yankees for six years beginning in 1998, says making the transition from Cuba to the major leagues was difficult. He cited the difficulties Jose Contreras had with the Yankees before becoming an All-Star with the Chicago White Sox.

"There are some good players in Cuba, but it is different here," he said. "You never know how somebody might do. Jose had a rough time at the start, but adjusted well.

"It's a different game here. You just never know how a player is going to react when he comes here."

"In 1911," according to a story in the August 5, 2002, *New Yorker*, "the Cincinnati Reds drafted two Cuban players, the first of more than a hundred to be recruited to the American major leagues over the next 50 years.

"In the 1940s and 1950s, some teams even had full-time scouts in Cuba. It has long been rumored that, in 1942, a scout working for the Washington Senators met with a promising teenage pitcher named Fidel Castro, a rangy right-hander with velocity but not technique.

"Castro claims that the team gave him a contract, which he turned down; baseball historians say the Senators never made him an offer. It has also been rumored that he passed on a $5,000 signing bonus from the New York Giants in order to go to law school. There is no dispute, however, that he remained passionate about the game.

"After the revolution, Castro banned most aspects of American popular culture, but baseball was so embedded in Cuba and his own life—he sometimes pitched for an exhibition team called the Bearded Ones—that it persisted and even expanded, although Castro remade it in to a revolutionary spirit.

"In 1961 (the year Oliva left the country for his major league career), Castro enacted National Decree 83A, which outlawed professional sports in Cuba.

"Henceforth, all competitive sports would be played by amateurs, the best of whom would receive a small government stipend equivalent to a worker's salary. This would end, as Castro took care to point out, American-style "slave baseball," in which players were bought and sold like property, and owners were enriched at the expense of the public.

"Cuban players would represent their home provinces, would never be traded, and would never get rich."

It should be pointed out that when Cuba won gold medals in the 1992 and 1996 Olympics they were celebrated as vindication of revolutionary baseball."

But when Coach Tommy Lasorda led the United States to victory in Sydney in 2000, it was regarded by Castro and Cuba as a calamity.

Oliva says when the Twins were still the Washington Senators, they were the first team to scout heavily in Cuba, where they signed three-time strikeout leader Camilo Pascual, as well as the 1965 AL MVP Zoilo Versalles.

As our conversation was winding down, I asked Oliva about some of his memorable experiences.

"Don't forget the 1966 All-Star Game in St. Louis," he said. "We were playing in the new Busch Stadium—it's since been demolished—and it had that artificial turf.

"I'll never forget it. The temperature was 105 degrees in the midday sun. We [American League] lost in 10 innings 2–1 and I played the whole game. I never like to lose, but when Tim McCarver scored the winning run in the 10th inning on a single by Maury Wills my feet were burning.

"It was the hottest day of my life—and I grew up in Cuba!"

Casey Stengel, retired, was sitting near home plate. When someone asked him what he thought of the new ballpark, he said, "It sure holds the heat well!"

Oliva still remains close to the Twins and works with their young players, especially the Latin players. He told me he knows how difficult an adjustment it is for them and he tries to make them feel as comfortable as possible.

Yes, it's been a long, but wonderful trip from Pinar del Rio, Cuba.

"The game of baseball is still the same," he said.

"But we just try to make it too difficult and that's a shame."

Change Is Good?

When the Red Sox handed out coveted World Series rings
from their 2013 championship over St. Louis, Bill
James was in the receiving line.

Yes, Bill James, baseball's original sabermetrician.

He received his ring because he's a senior advisor to the Red
Sox. During his tenure the Red Sox won the World Series in 2004,
2007, and 2013.

Consider this: James now has three World Series rings. Hall of
Famer Carl Yastrzemski never earned one.

Bill James is the most extreme example of how baseball invites
innovation, just as America has.

During the early 1990s, Bill and I appeared on the nationally
syndicated radio show *Baseball Sunday* from studios in Kansas City.
Bill and I often sparred over his radical ideas and his techniques
in rating and analyzing players. I called him a statistics guru; he
argued he's a sports journalist.

Joe Garagiola, the show's host, would frequently referee our
heated, but good-natured, arguments.

After spending all those hours with James I learned how gifted
he is, how important he has been to the game.

Bill rewrote how we see and measure baseball. His work has shaped the *Moneyball* era, the players it values, and even the Academy Award–nominated movie starring Brad Pitt as Oakland general manager Billy Beane.

Even the most devout purists agree baseball has been shaped by innovation.

Commissioner Bud Selig, a self-proclaimed purist, has been at the forefront of dramatic, and I must admit, enormously successful changes to the game.

Selig, who has announced he will retire on January 24, 2015, has led baseball since September 9, 1992.

During his regime many changes have been introduced, including the addition of two wild cards from each league for the postseason, interleague play, and the six-division format, as well as many other innovations, including extensive video replay.

Nothing has been more controversial than the ratification by the American League of the designated hitter in 1973. Believe it or not, the DH was first proposed within baseball in 1891.

It's become one of the most pivotal changes to our national pastime and has triggered criticism from those who oppose it and those who love it.

On September 3, 2008, I was at Tropicana Field in St. Petersburg when the Yankees' Alex Rodriguez hit a ninth-inning fly ball high over the left-field foul pole. It ricocheted off a catwalk above the field.

It was called a home run.

Rays manager Joe Maddon asked crew chief Charlie Reliford to review the call. Two minutes, 15 seconds later, after video replay was studied from the MLB Advanced Media headquarters in New York, the home run stood.

That is when replay, which only recently had been adopted, was used and became a part of Major League Baseball for the first time.

Nothing is more innovative than MLB utilizing modern technology to make sure the calls by umpires are correct.

It started in 2008 with just home run calls.

Beginning in 2014, expanded video replay is being utilized throughout Major League Baseball. Managers will be permitted to call for a replay in certain situations. The replays will be quickly studied from a bank of state-of-the-art monitors in MLB Advanced Media headquarters at 75 Ninth Avenue in New York and the findings relayed to umpires working the game in question.

Changes such as this are often difficult to accept.

The human element has been so important to baseball, there's always a danger when that is lessened.

But when you think of the technology available today and how it is so important crucial plays are called correctly, even devout purists agree video replay is necessary.

"Three or four years ago, I wasn't the least bit interested in expanded replay," Selig said recently. "Well, my father told me many years ago that life is nothing but a series of adjustments.

"And this is an adjustment that I've made."

Balls and strikes, check swings, and several other aspects of the game will not be involved.

"We do not want to lose sight of umpiring on the field," said Joe Torre, MLB executive vice president. "We have to make sure that umpiring on the field doesn't get punished by this. We may have replay, but that doesn't mean we're going to sacrifice the quality on the field."

Former manager Jim Leyland, a member of Selig's blue-ribbon committee for on-field matters, told me, "People have become so obsessed with getting the calls right. That's why they're doing what they're doing.

"I think they should replay some, but not to the extent that it is."

Innovation?

Doug Melvin, Milwaukee Brewers general manager has been in baseball as a player and an executive since 1972.

"I think we always have to be open-minded for something new," he told me. "In any business you do, in any sport, things have changed a lot. I do think there's a point where we do have to

take a step back sometimes and think, *Are the changes helping? Have they been effective?*

"There's no doubt there's a lot of growth in our game, there's more money in it than ever before. The thing we always have to be concerned about is it's still a game, a family event, family entertainment. We have to make sure we don't lose touch of that. And we don't lose touch of the history of the game."

In 2006, *Time* named Bill James in the *Time 100* as one of the most influential people in the world. He's appeared on the acclaimed *60 Minutes* to explain his theories.

James, a former schoolteacher and now 64, has always had a different approach.

He began writing baseball articles in his mid-twenties while doing night shifts as a security guard at the Stokely–Van Camp's pork-and-beans cannery in Kansas. That was after he returned home from the Vietnam War.

His stories didn't report baseball games as most writers do and there were no interviews with players.

What Bill did was inject a statistical analysis and his insights in the stories. He would ask a question, based on a stat, then answer it.

Most editors were cool to his approach. *Then.*

"I wanted to be a writer to begin with," James told me during an extensive December 2013 interview. "I'm an obsessive baseball fan. I still am, more so now than ever. I think about it all the time.

"I wake up in the middle of the night dreaming, always about baseball. It's just the central-organizing principle in my life."

In 1976, James had some articles published in *Baseball Digest.*

"And in the spring of 1977, I bought a bunch of the team annuals. I don't really know who wrote them, but as I read them, I thought, *I can do better than this.* I remember one particular example when they confused Joe Keough with Marty Keough— they weren't the same player. Little things like that. I just decided without any understanding how difficult it would be to start doing my own research in my own way and publish it myself.

"My operating assumption was, I don't know anything; I'm not in any way an expert, so anything I write I have to be able to show somebody it's true. So, I started doing things like counting the number of runs scored in support of each major league pitcher—just so that I would have some information that other people didn't have."

As long as I've known Bill, he's had a habit of playing down his expertise and it was no different as we talked about his early years as he attempted to get his approach off the ground.

"Everything I did, even in the beginning, is founded on the assumption that I'm not any kind of an expert. That's still true today," he said. "I still assume somebody else probably knows the game better than I do. What I say, I have to be able to prove is true or no one is going to believe it."

So, he self-published *The Bill James Baseball Abstract* in 1977. It consisted of 80 pages of in-depth statistics gleaned from his study of box scores from the 1976 season. He tried to sell it through an ad in *The Sporting News*.

"I had the first *Abstract* printed by a small publisher," he said. "They basically photocopied my pages. I sold the book out of my house four or five years. I can tell you this: I've never finished a book in my life without saying, 'This is the last one. It's too much work, I'm too tired, too beat up.'

"It's like when your wife has a baby. She always swears that's it, she cannot do it again."

Bill says the first *Abstract* sold 75 copies, the second about 300, the third 400, and the fifth about 2,000.

"It was my notion at that time there was a niche for me, if I could just reach about 4,000 readers and sell them a book every year, and make a five or seven-dollar profit on each one, I could make twice as much money as I was teaching school. That was my initial understanding how I could make a living doing what I love."

Eventually, James stopped teaching because "you cannot teach and write at the same time. Teaching requires all your energy."

He began publishing the *Abstract* yearly and by 1982 sales had increased enormously, so much so a national publisher agreed to publish and distribute his book.

Since then, he's written more than 30 books devoted to baseball history and statistics.

I asked Bill, in his words, to define what his true approach is.

"It's the search for the objective knowledge about baseball," he said. "What I do is listen carefully and try to find something that no one knows that could be known if you study it. That's what I have done my entire career."

Example?

"I remember Joe Morgan, at that time a player, saying it was easier to steal bases against a left-handed pitcher than against a right-handed pitcher. His reasoning was the left-hander was looking directly at you, but you also were looking at him. And you could see what he was doing.

"That's counterintuitive. Most people would think it's easier to steal on a right-hander because he cannot watch *you*. So, I thought I could study that—how many bases are stolen against left-handed and how many against right-handed pitchers."

Another example: It might be said a certain type of player ages well.

Bill then asks, "Is that true? So, I'll identify a hundred players, if there are a hundred of that type, 50 or whatever there are, and try to figure out whether they age better than players of the opposite type."

A year after a group headed by John Henry purchased the storied American League franchise, Bill James joined the Red Sox in November 2002 as senior baseball operations advisor.

According to the Red Sox, he works with senior management and the baseball operations group to provide research and analysis of special projects, player contracts, and "ongoing concerns."

His profile on Wikipedia states: "Although James is typically tight-lipped about his activities on behalf of the Red Sox, he is credited with advocating some of the moves that led to the team's first World Series championship in 86 years, its defeat of St. Louis in 2004.

"The signing of non-tendered free agent David Ortiz, the trade for Mark Bellhorn, and the team's increased emphasis on on-base percentage," were mentioned.

Bill agrees he has little to divulge about the information he provides the World Series champs, but loves his involvement.

"It's very rewarding," he said in an understatement.

After the Red Sox suffered through a disastrous last-place finish in 2012 under Bobby Valentine, Henry stated that James had fallen "out of favor in the front office of the last few years for reasons I really don't understand. We've gotten him more involved recently in the central process and that will help greatly."

Michael Lewis' book *Moneyball: The Art of Winning an Unfair Game* describes how the Athletics under Beane and Harvard economics grad Paul DePodesta used statistics to pick its ballplayers. The team's record was matched only by the Yankees, which had spent three times as much on talent.

In 2013, for example, Oakland's Opening Day payroll was 27th among the 30 teams at $60.8 million. That compares to the Yankees at $233.4 million and the $150.6 million of the champion Red Sox.

Beane became the Oakland general manager following the 1997 season.

Over the past 15 seasons, the A's have won six American League West titles and have posted 90 or more wins in eight of the last 14 years.

What made the numerical approach work so effectively is that few had paid attention to the mass of player data available in baseball. Scouts and managers who traditionally chose team rosters based decisions on gut feelings and assumptions they had learned as they came up in the game. But close analysis showed that certain types of traits and skills ignored by the "experts" better predicted who would win.

Moneyball is a book and a movie, but really a phenomenon.

Beane ended his six-year career as a major league outfielder in Oakland after the 1989 season. He was a utility player on the A's '89 championship team that swept San Francisco in the "Earthquake" World Series.

In 1990, he joined the A's front-office staff as the team's advance scout.

It was about then he became enamored with the work of Bill James and sabermetrics. To this day, Beane keeps some of James' typewritten, photocopied *Baseball Abstracts* in his office.

"I'll never throw them away," he says.

Bill James is admittedly flattered how his work is essentially the basis for Beane's approach to baseball, and the theme of *Moneyball.*

"It's an example of my whole career," said James. "Somebody's writing a book in which I'm a small character and it turns out to be a really good book and is made into a really good movie. That kind of break has come to me again and again. I feel so fortunate. I don't know why this is true, but the press has always been good to me."

James still publishes the *Bill James Handbook*. This publication provides past-season statistics and next-season projections for major league players and teams, and career data for all current major league players.

In November 2011, Simon Kuper of the *Financial Times* sat *Moneyball* author Michael Lewis and Beane down for a comprehensive, revealing discussion of how the book came to life, interwoven with an in-depth look into the Beane's sabermetrics philosophy.

Lewis said in 2001 he noticed that the Oakland A's were routinely beating teams with several times their budget.

As the two gained each other's trust, Lewis and Beane continually talked. And out of their conversations came *Moneyball*, the book. It has sold more than a million copies worldwide.

"Sabermetrics enchanted Beane," wrote Kuper.

"Anyone in baseball could have pinched James' ideas, but there are specific reasons—beyond Beane's personal journey—why the A's were there first.

"First, they had no money. As Brad Pitt tells his scouts in the movie, 'The problem we're trying to solve is there are rich teams, and there are poor teams.' He pauses, before adding: 'Then there is 50 feet of crap, then there's us.'

"The A's needed to find talent cheap. Second, the Coliseum is just a traffic jam away from the United States' most innovative region. 'We're in the shadow of Silicon Valley here,' marvels Beane. It's surely no coincidence that the hippies, the breakdown of the family, the high-five, the personal computer, Google, the iPhone, and Moneyball all came out of northern California."

Innovation became costly. After Billy Beane began using numbers to find players, the A's scouts lost their lifelong jobs. In the movie, one of them protests to Pitt (Beane): "You are discarding what scouts have done for 150 years."

Writes Kuper: "That was exactly right. Similar fates had been befalling all sorts of lesser-educated American men for years, though the process is more noticeable now than it was in 2003 when *Moneyball* first appeared."

Doug Melvin is concerned some of this has taken away key ingredients of the game.

"The history of baseball has made it the great game it is," he told me. "We used to have one trainer, now we have two trainers and it's up to three. We have conditioning coaches, doctors involved, nutritionists, but there are still more injuries than ever. Is that contracts being guaranteed, more agents involved?

"The players have more involvement with their agents than they do their ballclubs. As ballclubs, we're losing touch with our players."

Melvin adds: "You don't want to take the instincts away from the game. Baseball is played on instincts. The pace of the game has increased—guys are throwing harder, guys are faster, stronger. And yet we have all these systems put in place that you have to think, think. You just cannot take away the instincts.

"With the Fox Track and all that, even the instincts of the umpires have been taken away some.

"We've gone from one extreme to maybe the other. If it's helpful, we should move forward with it. But there comes a time when you have to take a step back and ask, 'Have all the improvements, advancements improved our game?'

"That's where you have to take a step back."

During a symposium at the Yogi Berra Museum late in 2013 that brought together five current and former managers, the subject of *Moneyball* came up. Numbers are important, all agreed, but the human element cannot be overlooked.

Orioles skipper Buck Showalter expressed concern that players think decisions are coming not from the manager, but from numbers.

Yankees manager Joe Girardi said: "I personally love numbers. That's my background. I love math, but I think you use the math to back up what you see, and I think at times, they use the numbers to try to prove a point.

"But it does support sometimes what you're trying to do. The one thing it doesn't do, it doesn't tell you about a guy's heart. And that's what you need to know if he's going to be successful in the long run, and if you want him in the trenches with you when the game gets tough."

Beane played for Tony La Russa when the latter was managing the Oakland A's, but Moneyball has no place in Tony's world.

"Michael Lewis wrote a nice story, it's got some truth to it, and Billy has taken that thing and made himself a fortune and I'm very upset about it," La Russa said.

La Russa believes there's a trend of teams relying on analytics to the point of dictating lineups and strategy to managers throughout their organizations.

"It's an arrogance for these people to stand there and tell guys in baseball that this is how you should run the game," he said. "It's arrogant and it's foolish, and if I managed again, I'd love to have five teams in the division using that process, and we'd clean their clock every day."

Nothing is more innovative or long-lasting in baseball than the box score.

We take it for granted. In fact, the term is used in many other sports as a summary of the event.

The *Dickson Baseball Dictionary* states that for years it was believed that the first box score appeared in the *New York Clipper* on July 16, 1853. "However, historian Melvin Adelman located a newspaper account of a baseball game in the *New York Herald* from October 25, 1845, accompanied by a sort of proto–box score that qualifies as a 'condensed statistical summary,' of the game," the Dickson dictionary states.

Box scores didn't appear with regularity in newspapers until 1876.

The term comes from the old newspaper custom of placing the data in a boxed-off section of the page.

Rule changes also fall under the category of innovation.

In March of 2014, Major League Baseball and the players association added rule 7.13, which essentially eliminates intentional collisions at home plate. It will be effective for the 2014 season on an experimental basis.

"Home-plate collisions are something you cannot ignore," said Torre.

Those who insist home-plate collisions have always been acceptable probably do not realize how the advancement of medical science has shown us how severe even the slightest of concussions can become in later years.

When Giants All-Star catcher Buster Posey suffered a broken bone in his left leg and three torn ligaments in his ankle during a collision with the Marlins' Scott Cousins in May 2011, discussions to ban collisions intensified.

"All that we know now about what's happening in any sport with collisions and concussions has to be examined, not only from the catcher's standpoint, but from the base runner's standpoint," says Giants GM Brian Sabean. "Do you really want anybody in harm's way? And should they allow there to be any malicious intent in baseball?"

Yankees GM Brian Cashman said: "I don't think catchers should be getting pounded."

There has never been a more memorable home-plate collision than Pete Rose crashing into Ray Fosse to score the winning run for the National League in the 1970 All-Star Game at Cincinnati's Riverfront Stadium. Fosse suffered a dislocated shoulder and was never the same player.

With 2014's rule change, plays like Rose-Fosse will never happen again.

Some say that's innovation; some say it's erosion. Ruining a great game or making it better? The conventional wisdom is that only time will tell, but sometimes even time isn't enough. Let me show you:

Did the addition of the designated hitter pervert the beautiful strategy of baseball, or is it a common-sense change that makes the game more fun?

See.

16

The Big Job

Kenesaw Mountain Landis was the first.

He was appointed Commissioner of Baseball, the sport's first, on November 12, 1920, and paid $50,000 a year to fix the game's greatly damaged reputation.

The Black Sox scandal, when eight White Sox players, including Shoeless Joe Jackson, conspired to throw the 1919 World Series to the Cincinnati Reds, destroyed the credibility of baseball.

The White Sox lost the series to the Reds, and the Chicago players were later accused of intentionally losing games in exchange for money from gamblers. Those players were acquitted in court, but nevertheless, they were all banned for life from organized baseball.

Landis, a federal judge since 1905, was given full power to act in baseball's best interest, and used that power extensively over the next quarter-century.

Judge Landis was a czar in every sense of the word.

Allan Huber Selig was appointed interim commissioner on September 9, 1992. When the Milwaukee Brewers owner accepted that assignment—on a temporary basis—baseball was in dreadful shape. Commissioner Fay Vincent had been forced out of office and frankly, baseball at the highest level was a shambles. It was a chaotic mess.

Selig's assignment?

Keep the sinking ship afloat. Try to bring unity to a fractured ownership group.

From the time Landis died in office on November 25, 1944, at age 78, he'd ruled the game for 22 years.

From that date to Bud Selig's taking the wheel, there were seven commissioners: Happy Chandler (1945–1951), Ford Frick (1951–1965), William D. Eckert (1965–68), Bowie Kuhn (1969–1984), Peter Ueberroth (1984–1989), Bart Giamatti (1989), and Vincent (1989–1992).

Chandler, who'd been the governor of Kentucky and a U.S. Senator, followed Landis. He resigned after major league owners refused to renew his contract for a second seven-year term.

When I read his comments in his 1989 autobiography, *Heroes, Plain Folks and Skunks*, the words might have come out of the mouth of most any commissioner who battled owners.

"Many of the owners were greedy," Chandler wrote. "They were cruel to the players and the umpires. They abused the fans. They tried to dominate me. I banished Leo 'The Lip' Durocher for a full year for besmirching the game. I just didn't sit around. For the first time players got pensions and a fair shake on rights, pay and contracts. I helped integrate baseball. The avaricious owners began to boil. They finally greased the skids and railroaded me out."

Owners then didn't appreciate commissioners who spoke their mind.

In Jerome Holtzman's 1998 book *The Commissioners,* the late Gabe Paul, who owned or operated four major league teams, said this about Chandler: "Happy was a good commissioner but he talked a lot. If he hadn't talked so much he wouldn't have gotten into so much trouble."

In my 55-plus years covering Major League Baseball, I've had contact with or interviewed everyone except Landis and Chandler.

I liked Bowie Kuhn. We had a good working relationship. I believe Bowie's biggest problem was Marvin Miller, the aggressive executive director of the Major League Players Association. Kuhn appeared helpless during the players' strike of 1981. He just wasn't about to bring about a labor settlement without a work stoppage of some type.

He stayed on for 15 years and was replaced by Peter Ueberroth, the financial whiz who ran the 1984 Los Angeles Summer Olympics, a job that earned him *Time* magazine's coveted Man of the Year honor.

When Ueberroth was hired to replace Kuhn, major league owners felt he was perfect to put baseball on solid financial footing. He was supposed to show management how to increase revenues with lower player costs.

Peter will always be known as the "collusion" commissioner. Owners were found guilty of colluding and not signing some of the game's top players who'd become free agents.

That arbitrator's decision cost the owners $280 million—the largest fine in professional sports history. Ueberroth didn't finish his term and left in March 1989.

As Ueberroth was preparing to leave as commissioner he engineered a then staggering TV deal in excess of $1.2 billion with CBS.

I sat at a table with Ueberroth during a media briefing following an owners meeting in Fort Lauderdale.

Ueberroth was proud of the TV contract.

"There's no way now owners can bankrupt themselves," he remarked. "There's now plenty of money."

Ueberroth was wrong. Within months almost every dollar had been spent—on player salaries. Average salary more than doubled during the term of the deal, from $489,000 to $1 million.

When CBS realized it had overspent and asked for a refund, baseball said the money was all gone.

Ueberroth was replaced by the eloquent National League president A. Bartlett Giamatti, former Yale president. Bart, a Renaissance man, loved baseball. He took office in April 1989, and after banning Pete Rose for life in August for gambling on baseball, died a week later from a massive heart attack. He was succeeded by his deputy, Fay Vincent.

Selig, the owner, was very close to Giamatti. I always held the opinion that Giamatti could have been a great commissioner, had he lived long enough.

From the day Selig became interim commissioner, I repeatedly predicted he'd not step aside for someone else. If there really was a search, in my mind it seemed to always come full-circle to Selig.

This wasn't an ego thing. It was his unbelievable passion for baseball and his background telling him during this troubled era no one could do the job better. He knew the game and people in it—the good, the bad, the skeletons, and all the hidden agendas. An outsider would have drowned like someone in quicksand.

For the better part of three decades baseball had changed very little. For previous commissioners, it was merely status quo. But as Bud Selig told me, "Baseball was stuck in neutral. Pro football went by us like a jet. The sport needed fixing at many levels."

The search committee in the 1990s that was appointed to find a permanent commissioner was a charade. There was never anyone but Bud Selig. He was unanimously elected to the post during an owners meeting at the Chicago O'Hare Hilton on July 9, 1998.

Selig, now 79, said on September 26, 2013, that he'll retire upon completion of his current contract on January 24, 2015.

We've heard that many times in the past and he may stick to his word, but I doubt it.

During a long interview for this book, I asked him if he's really sincere about leaving.

"I have really thought to myself it's time, it really is," he said.

I mentioned there are people who think he'll stay on if the owners ask him to.

"I know people are saying a lot of things," he said, "but I'm smart enough to know there comes a time in life when you have to get out of the way."

And then, he left the door open: "Listen, I'll always do what the owners want me to do. I always will. We haven't even discussed this stuff [staying on] yet, but I'm here to help. I think it's important; I'm here to do whatever needs to be done."

There have been bumps in the road for Selig, including the devastating 1994–95 players strike, which caused the cancellation of the '94 World Series.

Did he act quickly enough when steroids became the game's biggest problem?

Critics insist those issues should be part of his legacy.

But even with that, Selig has done more to improve baseball than any of his predecessors.

So, here it is: Allan H. Selig is the best commissioner baseball has ever had.

And if he does walk away in January 2015, his replacement will face a Herculean task measuring up.

Philadelphia Phillies chairman Bill Giles, son of the late National League president Warren Giles, has known every commissioner since the first, Judge Landis.

"Bud has done more for baseball than any commissioner before him," says Giles, who admits he wasn't pleased with Selig in the beginning.

During the 21 years he's been in office, Selig accomplished more than all of the previous eight commissioners combined.

When he assumed leadership in 1992, MLB's total revenue was $1.2 billion; today it is more than $8 billion, an increase of more than 650 percent. In 2012, the Los Angeles Dodgers sold for more than $2 billion, much more than twice the price for any previous franchise.

The average franchise value, according to *Forbes* magazine, is $744 million. The Yankees franchise alone is worth $2.3 billion.

When I think back to the eight work stoppages I covered beginning in 1972, that Selig has been able to usher in an era of unprecedented labor peace could be his biggest achievement.

By the time the current Collective Bargaining Agreement expires in 2016, Major League Baseball will have had a period of 21 years without a labor interruption.

Doris Kearns Goodwin, a renowned author and historian said: "Generations from now students of baseball will look back with wonder at the astonishing number of significant reforms instituted under Commissioner Selig's leadership. The combination of an expanded postseason and wild-card berths has resulted in more teams playing October baseball than ever before, keeping the interest of millions of fans alive when summer turns to fall.

"When Spring Training begins, more fans in more cities can now realistically hope that their beloved team has a good chance to carry their dreams all the way to the end of the season. What this has done to keep the heart of baseball alive is simply immeasurable."

Selig is always telling me how much competitive balance has improved. Nine different teams have won the last 13 World Series and 26 of the 30 teams have been to the postseason over the last decade.

Selig's legacy also includes the canceling of the 1994 World Series during the players strike and the evolution of the steroid era. He goes to great lengths to defend what has been widely described as the game's slow reaction to the steroid issue, saying he is convinced he could not have acted earlier or done things differently.

After the single-season home run record fell twice in four years, MLB conducted anonymous survey testing in 2003. Mandatory testing started the following year. The policy was strengthened before the season in 2005 and 2006, when amphetamines were added to the banned list and a third positive test could result in a lifetime ban.

The program has gotten even stronger.

"Look, we got a testing program, tightened it once, tightened it twice, changed it again. Where are we now? The toughest program in American professional sports," Selig says. "We've banned amphetamines, put in HGH blood tests. A team trainer and doctor told me if we didn't do something about amphetamines somebody was going to die.

"A writer said to me the other day, 'Why should you have known? You're never in the clubhouses. I was there every day, and I didn't know.' And that's exactly what the general managers tell me."

Lew Wolff, owner of the Oakland Athletics, was a year behind Selig at Wisconsin. They belonged to the same fraternity, and their college friendship has extended over the years. "Bud was the president [of our fraternity, Pi Lambda Phi]. Some of his techniques he used then are similar to those he uses with owners," Wolff says. "When I reflect back, he seemed to mature a lot faster than most of us."

You can talk about the improved revenues, labor peace, the addition of interleague play, the new wild-card teams, the most comprehensive and aggressive drug and treatment program in professional sports, but really, what is Bud Selig all about?

We see him on TV with his unkempt hair and, honestly, not appearing as the perfect or suave image of a baseball commissioner. Yet few sports executives are more candid, more honest, more accessible, or more friendly than Selig.

Richard Levin, who retired several years ago as MLB's public relations vice president, puts it this way: "There's an 'everyman' quality to Bud Selig, which may be one of the reasons why people tend to underestimate him. Another may be that he chooses to live and work in Milwaukee, well outside the big media centers of New York, Los Angeles and Chicago.

"Those who do underestimate him live to regret it, because Bud is a brilliant man, a master politician, and an unrelenting salesman. Much to the chagrin of those who work for and with him, he never forgets. But he's quick to forgive. He rarely holds a grudge. He's one of a kind."

Although the so-called steroids era occurred on his Selig's watch, once he became aware of the magnitude and importance of the problem, he has taken extraordinary steps to resolve the issue and has made it his mission to make every effort to eradicate the use of performance-enhancing substances from the game. So much so that today, Major League Baseball, by far, has the toughest drug testing program among all the professional sports. And, he has made it clear that he will go after all offenders, regardless of their stature in the game.

During his term 21 new ballparks have been built, there is greater competitive balance in baseball than in the other professional sports, the game is more popular than ever before,and the World Baseball Classic has brought the game to new fans throughout the global market.

"And there is no doubt labor peace is the singular reason Major League Baseball has enjoyed the greatest success it has, both on and off the field, over the past two decades," says Levin.

Toronto Blue Jays CEO Paul Beeston said, "He's done a tremendous job for the game. I don't know anybody else who would put in the hours he does. I'm amazed. Really, he relaxes with his job. When he's not got something on his mind that is baseball related, at that time I don't think he's relaxed. His relaxation is his vocation."

Levin said, "Bud often speaks about how baseball is a social institution with important social responsibilities. This isn't a public relations gambit. He takes this responsibility seriously as he has shown on numerous occasions.

"In 1997, on the 50th anniversary of Jackie Robinson's entry into Major League Baseball, Selig directed all teams to retire Jackie's No. 42 in perpetuity throughout the game. He said that

that day—April 15, 1947—was baseball's proudest and most important moment.

"He's often pointed out that Jackie integrated baseball while much of America was separate and unequal, stating that Jackie broke down baseball's color barrier a couple of years before Harry Truman integrated the United States Army, seven years before the Supreme Court handed down the historic *Brown v. Board of Education* decision, before the courageous Rosa Parks defied authorities and rightfully took a seat near the front of the bus, and long before Dr. Martin Luther King and the Civil Rights Movement woke up America and put real meaning behind the words, 'All men are created equal.'"

George F. Will, who wrote the baseball best-seller *Men at Work,* said: "Bud Selig, together with Babe Ruth and Jackie Robinson, has had one of baseball's three most consequential careers. Since 1992, baseball has gained 21 new ballparks, interleague play, realignment of the leagues into three divisions, two wild cards that have multiplied the number of meaningful games played in September, and a prudent embrace of technologies.

"Furthermore, MLB's transformed economic model has produced competitive balance unprecedented in major league history and unmatched in other professional sports leagues. The game's robust attendance figures testify to all these improvements."

Selig has often said how important commissioners are to baseball. Not only was he a history major in college, he's a history buff. He's studied each of the previous commissioners and mentally filed away where they succeeded, where they failed.

What he has done is make this job become more successful for him than any of the others because he knew what the game needed when he took over.

He's been criticized for being a former owner, but I believe this gave him a huge edge because he knew first-hand what the problems were. He knew the other owners—those who'd come aboard with progressive change, those who'd fight it.

I learned early in Selig's regime that building consensus was his greatest talent.

But he was smart enough not to put any issue up for a vote by owners until he knew in advance what the final score would be.

Bud Selig would never be blindsided.

"I'm not going to get personal about other commissioners, but I've been fortunate," he told me. "I love the game and I've studied it all my life. I came into baseball under Bowie Kuhn, so I had him to watch, I had Peter Ueberroth to watch.

"I am a student of American history and baseball history. I studied Judge Landis, I studied Ford Frick, and I've been witness to most of them."

Selig refused to discuss Vincent, and although he was close to and respected Bart Giamatti, he died so soon after taking office in 1989 that his record was very short.

"I truly believe I have a really clear understanding of how the job has changed, who did what and when. And it's helped me to understand the very job that I've had now since 1992."

Vincent, who succeeded Giamatti, did a solid job in the beginning. He handled the 1989 San Francisco–earthquake World Series well. After a 10-day hiatus as the Bay Area worked to heal and regroup, the Series was resumed.

Later in Vincent's tenure, I believe he thought he was bigger than the game itself. The owners were not comfortable with him negotiating a new collective bargaining agreement, so Richard Ravitch was brought in at $750,000 a year—$100,000 more than Vincent's salary.

With him removed from labor negotiations, I believe his days were numbered, especially after he continued to alienate a group of owners who wanted him out of office.

"I knew back in 1992, once I began to access all the damage, and then '93, '94, '95, I knew how fractured the sport was for 50 years," said Selig. "It was worse in the 1980s and the 1970s.

"I remember saying to myself that if I was going to accomplish what was needed, this group [of owners] was going to have to get together," he said. "It couldn't have the fractions that existed. You just couldn't have that.

"I set about to do that—big market, small market, medium market—it didn't matter to me. We'd been stuck for three decades. We needed to move forward."

Revenue sharing was the hot-button topic then. It became a battle between big markets and small markets. The richest teams were opposed to helping the small markets—á la revenue sharing.

I attended what turned out to be a crucial owners meeting at the posh American Club in Kohler, Wisconsin, about 50 miles north of Milwaukee, on August 13, 1993.

Ravitch discussed the importance of ownership finalizing a revenue-sharing plan that could be presented to the players union so that management's salary cap could be adopted.

The owners began meeting at noon. They met through dinner.

The *Milwaukee Journal's* Tom Haudricort, who has a tremendous sense of humor, remarked: "The dinner menu is lobster thermidor for the big-market operators. And the small-market guys are saying, 'Give us some of your lobster and we'll give you half of our ham sandwich.'"

The next day the big-market owners separated themselves from the small-market teams.

The Kohler meeting ended with a stalemate. I detail this session because a year later, on August 12, 1994, the players went on strike because there was no labor agreement.

I asked Selig if this was the low point of his attempt to bring unity to ownership in baseball.

"We had a lot of low points before then, but under my tutelage, Kohler was the low point," Selig said. "We were at rock bottom. We had to change the economics of the sport. It was obvious that disparity had set in. We were living in the Ebbets Field, Polo Grounds days. There had not been a change since the 1930s and '40s.

"To do that, I had to get people to understand why we were going to do it, how we were going to do it, and what we were going to do. As fractured as the sport was then and had been for a long time, that's how good it's been the last 15 to 20 years."

Selig is the ultimate baseball purist.

Yet he's the commissioner who introduced interleague play, added two wild cards, and two additional rounds to the postseason. In 2008 limited video replay was added for home-run calls. In 2014, replay will be dramatically expanded *and* there will be rules that forbid a runner to crash into a catcher when trying to score.

Selig even forced Houston to move from the National League to the AL in 2013, so each of the two leagues would have 15 teams.

Selig the purist?

"I'm proud of the changes we've made," he said, still proclaiming to be a purist. "What I knew is that everything in life has to make adjustments. My father used to say, 'Life is nothing but a series of adjustments.'

"And I'm a traditionalist as much as you are. I romanticize the game, and it was the game I grew up loving in the 1940s and 1950s. But I knew there had to be some changes, some economic changes, sociological changes, and changes on the field with rules.

"What we have done has worked and I'm convinced that's why the sport is more popular today than ever before. Our attendance the last six or seven years was stunning."

For Selig, the most difficult time was "all the labor heartache, and losing a World Series—those were just stunningly bad times for everybody.

"The 1994 World Series? *The players were out on strike.* They said, 'Well, you called off the World Series.' I had to announce to the American public we were on strike and we couldn't play. Dave Montgomery of the Phillies and Boston's John Harrington called me and said because of all the ticket issues, 'You've got to make an announcement.'

"We had 30 years of labor strife that was unproductive— Bowie Kuhn vs. Marvin Miller, Don Fehr and me. I knew then it was hurting us. You can see what all these years of labor peace has done. Everybody is better off—the players, the fans, the owners, and most importantly, the game."

Selig said the relationship with the players union has never been better.

"When Michael Weiner [union executive director] died last year [2013], it was a very sad time for us. It broke my heart."

When folks write Selig's legacy, it must be said he put the game above its superstars.

It mattered not that Ryan Braun and Alex Rodriguez were two of baseball's best-known and highest-paid players. They violated baseball's drug policy and were punished.

On a day—August 5, 2013—filled with recrimination, regret, and refrain, 13 players were penalized as a result of MLB's six-month-plus investigation of Biogenesis of America, a Florida anti-aging clinic accused of distributing banned performance-enhancing drugs.

Twelve accepted 50-game suspensions in baseball's most sweeping punishment since the Black Sox scandal nearly a century ago.

Alex Rodriguez was suspended through 2014, a total of 211 games, but was the lone player to appeal. Arbitrator Fredric Horowitz later reduced the suspension to 162 games, a full season.

With Ryan Braun's 65-game suspension in July 2013, the number of players connected to Biogenesis rose to 18.

The harshest penalty was reserved for Rodriguez, the New York Yankees slugger, a three-time Most Valuable Player and baseball's highest-paid star.

"I said in the very beginning, even before the Mitchell Report was commissioned, that we would have the toughest drug and treatment program in professional sports," said Selig. "Today, I am convinced we do."

Longtime author John Thorn, now MLB's official historian said: "No commissioner has faced greater challenges in defending and growing the game, not even Judge Landis. Selig has this unbiased observer's vote as the greatest of all baseball's chief executives."

In a sense, baseball is America.

"The game transcends all of us and you can never forget that," Selig said. "From the time I was a kid, the respect for the game and my passion for it is obvious [to] everyone who knows me.

"I'm honored to be the custodian for this generation. That's the best way I can say it."

17

There Used
to Be a Ballpark

I can still hear Frank Sinatra's unmistakable voice, crooning…
And there used to be a ballpark where the field was warm and green, and the people played their crazy game with a joy I'd never seen. And the air was such a wonder from hot dogs and the beer, yes, there used to be a ballpark right here.

It was October 6, 1950. My first trip to Yankee Stadium. My father had taken me there to watch the Yankees and Phillies play Game 3 of the World Series. Yes, that was a long, long time ago, but the memory of that baseball cathedral remains so vivid.

Joe DiMaggio walked to the plate to bat against Ken Heintzelman and my dad whispered in my ear, "Pay close attention. You'll be remembering this moment the rest of your life."

And now *my* Yankee Stadium, which opened in 1923, has given way to a new, billion-dollar state-of-the-art edifice, also fittingly called Yankee Stadium, but it can never replace the memories and the historic moments spent at Babe Ruth's house.

I covered my first World Series there in 1958, the Yankees vs. the Milwaukee Braves.

It took seven games for the Yankees to prevail. To win, they had to overcome the pitching heroics of Warren Spahn, who won two games before losing Game 6, 4–3 in 10 innings. Spahn gave up four runs and just nine hits in 9⅔ innings. It's unheard of today that a starting pitcher would last that far into a game.

In all, I've reported on 16 World Series at Yankee Stadium, three All-Star Games, and myriad playoff battles.

I cherish the times spent with the Boss there. George Steinbrenner was always good for a story, an opinion, a hug, or a hand shake. He is dearly missed.

Don Larsen threw his perfect game in the 1956 World Series on that field and there was Roger Maris and Lou Gehrig and Whitey Ford and Mickey Mantle and Casey Stengel and Billy Martin and Derek Jeter and Mariano Rivera, and of course, Mr. October.

My memory is vivid from that crisp night in 1977 when Reggie Jackson homered on the first pitch of three consecutive at-bats against three different Los Angeles Dodgers pitchers.

And it was on May 14, 1967, when Mantle crushed his 500th career home run.

And all the Old-Timers Games, just to refresh some memories, or walk through the Monument Park that commemorates 20 Yankee greats—players, managers, executives.

There was never a more storied sports palace in the land where grown men played a boy's game. I miss it.

And there used to be rock candy and a big Fourth of July with the fireworks exploding all across the summer sky. And the people watched in wonder; how they'd laugh and how they'd cheer, and there used to be a ballpark right here.

And there was Shibe Park, where Connie Mack, in his dark suit and starched white shirt, directed his Athletics.

And later it became Connie Mack Stadium, where the Phillies played the 1950 World Series and in 1964 lived through one of Major League Baseball's greatest collapses.

The old ballpark at 21st and Lehigh Avenues in north Philadelphia closed on a cold autumn night in 1970, stepping aside for the cookie-cutter Veterans Stadium.

As the park closed on October 1, there was virtual bedlam within. Once, in the sixth inning, as outfielder Ron Stone was trying to make a catch, a fan rushed onto the field and grabbed him. Seats were torn apart as souvenirs.

I remember one of the most hilarious sights: a fan carrying a toilet down Lehigh Avenue hours after the game.

Sadly, the deserted stadium burned in 1971 and was razed in 1976.

Memories…

Phillies Hall of Famer Richie Ashburn once said, "It looked like a ballpark. It smelled like a ballpark. It had a feeling and a heartbeat, a personality that was all baseball."

And now Veterans Stadium, its replacement, is only a parking lot that is looked down upon by the shiny new Citizens Bank Park.

And Ebbets Field, with all its history, is just a memory. So is Forbes Field and the Polo Grounds and Crosley Field, and Briggs Stadium and Sportsman's Park and Washington's Griffith Stadium, where I covered one of my first games in 1959.

The Polo Grounds was torn apart on April 10, 1964, by the same wrecking ball that leveled Ebbets Field in 1960.

Close your eyes. There's Willie Mays making the greatest catch in World Series history in center field at the Polo Grounds during the 1954 World Series.

Or Jackie Robinson on April 15, 1947, playing first base for the Dodgers at Ebbets Field, breaking baseball's rigid color barrier.

So many of these legendary ballparks are gone now, but the memories linger.

After the last out, they tell everybody to go home, flick off the lights, shut the doors, and turn their backs on these great sports venues. And it's a shame.

Now the children try to find it and they can't believe their eyes, 'cause the old team isn't playing and the new team hardly tries. And the sky has got so cloudy when it used to be so clear, and the summer went so quickly this year.

There are so many ballparks that live on only with cherished memories—memories that thankfully just won't go away.

Former Detroit Tigers outfielder Willie Horton still can't bear to drive by what used to be Tiger Stadium without crying.

There's a church pulpit where first base used to be at Shibe Park in Philadelphia.

In St. Louis, people stop daily to play catch in an open space at the YMCA, the old right field where Stan Musial used to play.

Pittsburgh still has the wall that Bill Mazeroski cleared for his famous homer in 1960 at Forbes Field that won the World Series over the Yankees.

I wonder what life's like for the folks who live in the Brooklyn apartments where Ebbets Field once stood.

In Cincinnati, there's a service station in what used to be Crosley Field's center field. People stop by to sit in seats from the former ballpark.

But Fenway Park and Wrigley Field remain, refusing to bow to the often ridiculous notion that new is better.

When I sit in the press box at Fenway Park today, it's like a journey into baseball's glorious past.

Oh, the players no longer wear baggy wool uniforms and there are the trappings of new, with a giant color video screen, music blaring over a high-tech sound system, and as many innovations and fan amenities as can possibly be crammed into a ballpark that celebrated its 101st birthday in 2013.

There's the legendary Green Monster in left field, the 37-foot-tall wall, a towering structure that is as much a part of Fenway Park lore as the "Curse of the Bambino."

The "curse" became superstition because the Red Sox were unable to win a World Series from 1918 until 2004 because Babe Ruth was sold to the Yankees.

And in right field, it's the Pesky Pole, the foul pole that was named after Johnny Pesky.

There are so many nooks at crannies at Fenway Park that frequently create nightmares for players during their first games there.

Yes, there are memories.

It was there that Babe Ruth was the winning pitcher in his major league debut on July 11, 1914. Ted Williams played his entire career at Fenway, as did Carl Yastrzemski and many others.

It was there I watched the Red Sox rally in Game 6 of the 1975 World Series as Carlton Fisk blasted his dramatic 12th-inning homer against Cincinnati. The Big Red Machine came back the next night to win the championship—the best World Series I've covered.

It was there the Impossible Dream of 1967 was etched. Yastrzemski won the Triple Crown as the Red Sox, under demanding manager Dick Williams, rebounded from a dreadful 1966 season to win the American League pennant with a 92–70 record before losing to St. Louis in the World Series.

Yes, it was 2004 when the Red Sox lost the first three games to the majestic Yankees in the American League Championship Series, only to come back and win four straight, then sweep the Cardinals in the World Series.

The Curse of the Bambino was gone, but Fenway Park remains.

About 1,025 miles to the west are the hallowed grounds of Wrigley Field, the Friendly Confines at the corner of Clark and Addison Streets on Chicago's North Side.

Is the wind blowing out today?

It had to be on August 25, 1922, when the Cubs edged the Phillies 26–23 in the highest-scoring game ever played. The two teams collected 51 hits, a record for a nine-inning game.

Shhh! Listen closely. Is that Harry Caray, waving his arms and leading Cubs fans in the singing of "Take Me Out to the Ball Game"?

Or Mr. Cub, Ernie Banks, proclaiming, "Let's play two!"

Banks, now a Hall of Famer, once said, "Wrigley is like another home in the community. When you're in Wrigley Field it's like you're visiting the family of all the people that live around here."

Ah, yes, beloved Wrigley Field, with its ivy-covered walls and long-starved faithful. Hey, the Cubbies have been trying since 1908 to win a World Series. But Wrigley Field, which opened in 1914, with the gales blowing off Lake Michigan, endures.

It was there that Stan Musial doubled to collect his 3,000[th] hit on May 13, 1958, and I was in the tiny, crowded press box when Pete Rose tied Ty Cobb's all-time career hits record of 4,191 on September 8, 1985.

I remember how nervous Reds officials were that Pete would collect another hit and shatter the record before returning to Riverfront Stadium in front of a cheering home crowd.

It was also there, during the 1932 World Series, Cubs vs. Yankees, that Babe Ruth supposedly called his home run. He allegedly pointed to center field to indicate he would hit a home run, and then delivered.

"I'd pay half my salary if I could bat in this dump all the time," Ruth was quoted as saying during that Series.

And the wind was definitely swirling out on May 17, 1979, when I watched Mike Schmidt and Bob Boone lead a home run barrage as the Phillies, with a firestorm of 24 hits, held off the Cubs 23–22 in 10 innings.

In 1958, the Brooklyn Dodgers and New York Giants moved to California.

Their departure signaled the last rites for Ebbets Field and the Polo Grounds.

In California, until the magnificent Dodger Stadium was built, the Dodgers played in the Los Angeles Coliseum for their first four years there. It could seat 90,000 for baseball and on April 18, 1958, the team's West Coast opener, 78,672 were on hand to see the Dodgers beat their rival Giants 6–5.

My first trip for baseball on the West Coast was later in 1958, and I was amazed at how close the left-field fence at the Coliseum was—just 250 feet from home plate!

They put up a 40-foot screen hopefully to reduce the number of home runs, but during that first season, 182 were hit to left field.

In San Francisco, while the Giants were waiting for Candlestick Park to be built, they played at Seals Stadium, a former minor league park.

I was in awe during my first visit there because just six years before Joe DiMaggio set his consecutive games hitting streak of 56 in 1941 he was in the minors, playing the outfield at Seals Stadium.

Memories…

Candlestick Park opened on April 12, 1960, and Dodger Stadium, still one of the gems of Major League Baseball, came to life on April 10, 1962.

Baseball moved indoors in 1965 when Houston's Astrodome opened.

People said that the Astros president, Judge H. Roy Hofheinz, who had been Houston's mayor and a county judge, was out of his mind when he announced plans for the Astrodome. He called it the "Eighth Wonder of the World," and in a sense, it was.

I watched the first game there on April 12, 1965, when the Phillies shut out the Astros 2–0. Richie Allen hit the first home run there and Chris Short was the winning pitcher.

I covered many games at the Astrodome, including the Philadelphia Phillies amazing 1980 National League Championship Series victory over the Astros.

A game on June 10, 1974, also stands out.

Mike Schmidt launched a gigantic shot that bounced off a speaker on the roof, falling back into the field of play. Schmidt was held to just a single. Folks talked about this for years, insisting had the ball not struck the speaker it would have traveled over 500 feet.

After the Astrodome, which closed in 1999, other indoor palaces followed: Seattle's Kingdome (1977), the Minneapolis Metrodome (1982), Toronto's SkyDome (1989), and Tropicana Field in St. Petersburg (1998).

Now, there are new ballparks with retractable roofs in Seattle, Phoenix, Miami, Milwaukee, and Houston.

With the influx of "retro" parks throughout major league baseball that began on April 6, 1992, with the opening of Oriole Park at Camden Yards, the emphasis has been on re-creating the charm of the old friendly venues that meant so much to the fabric of the game.

In Curt Smith's outstanding 2001 book *Storied Stadiums*, he quotes the late A. Bartlett Giamatti, National League president at the time, who said in 1988, "What I don't understand is the lack of imagination in ballpark design. Why can't we build an angular, idiosyncratic park for a change, with all the amenities and conveniences, and still make it better than anything we have."

That is exactly what baseball did.

Giamatti, who later became commissioner, was on-target when he predicted after seeing the plans for Camden Yards: "When this park is complete, every team is going to want one."

Giamatti, who died in 1989, did not live to see the opening of the fabulous Baltimore park.

The renaissance of baseball parks throughout the major leagues followed Camden Yards—Progressive Field, Target Field, Coors Field, Comerica Park, AT&T Park, Minute Maid Park, PNC Park, Great American Ball Park, PETCO Park, Citizens Bank Park, Nationals Park, Marlins Park, et al.

Obviously, these new multi-million-dollar parks have succeeded. In essence, they have taken baseball back to the future.

There's no contest when they're compared to the myriad "cookie cutter" stadiums that were built in the 1960s and '70s. Thankfully, they're long gone.

Phillies first baseman Richie Hebner once said, "When I stand at home plate at Veterans Stadium, I don't honestly know whether I'm in Cincinnati, Pittsburgh, St. Louis, or Philadelphia."

The concrete doughnuts were all the same.

When New York Mets owner Fred Wilpon—who grew up in Brooklyn not far from Ebbets Field—planned the new park to replace Shea Stadium he insisted the exterior of Citi Field be reminiscent of the place he worshipped as a youngster.

Citi Field, which opened in 2009, has arched windows and stone materials much like those at Ebbets. Wilpon, after obtaining the old blueprints of Ebbets Field, had architects design the rotunda much like that of his beloved park. It was named Jackie Robinson Rotunda.

The new ballparks are magnificent, tremendous drawing cards for their fans.

They've replaced so many wonderful, historic arenas. Arenas that are gone, but not forgotten.

Yes, there used to be a ballpark right here.

Acknowledgments

For 25 years, I was fortunate to first be a founding editor for *USA TODAY*, then its baseball editor/columnist until retirement in December 2007. Many of the interviews and anecdotes included in this book took place during my quarter of a century at the nation's newspaper. I cannot go any further without mentioning the enormous mentoring the late Al Neuharth provided for me. He's greatly missed.

Since January 2008, I've been the senior correspondent at MLB Advanced Media (MLB.com). I cannot thank Dinn Mann and Richard Bush enough for their guidance and support.

I would especially like to thank Jesse Jordan at Triumph Books for his advice, not to mention tireless and skillful editing of the manuscript. Also, Tom Bast of Triumph Books for making this project possible.

Without the exhausting assistance from Tim Wiles and Bill Francis from the library of the Baseball Hall of Fame and Museum this project would have been very lacking. Also, Hall of Fame president Jeff Idelson for lending a hand.

Special thanks to Bob Kuenster, *Baseball Digest* editor.

The cooperation and encouragement from these folks cannot be understated: Buddy Bell, Aaron Boone, Bob Boone, Dr. Bobby

Brown, Mary Burns, George H.W. Bush, George W. Bush, Cal & Diane Carrier, Albert T. Cartwright, Mary Casalino, Terry Cashman, the late Jerry Coleman, Leonard S. Coleman Jr., Pat Corrales, Bob Costas, Pat Courtney, Bobby Cox, Kirstyn Crawford, Pam Davis, Pearl Del Collo, Donald Fehr, Terry Francona, Henry Freeman, Joe Garagiola, Bill Giles, Dallas & Sylvia Green, John Hart, Rickey Henderson, Clint Hurdle, Phil Iannelli, Bill James, Tony La Russa, Tommy Lasorda, Richard Levin, Jim Leyland, Bill Madden, Joe Maddon, Charlie Manuel, Tim McCarver, Doug Melvin, Phyllis Merhige, Frankie Monzo, Joe Morgan, Tony Oliva, Eddie Robinson, Frank Robinson, Jimmy Rollins, Terry Ryan, Scott Sanderson, Allan H. "Bud" Selig, Todd Shaw, John Shea, Larry Shenk, Jim Slattery, Dr. Theodosios Soldatos, Jayson Stark, Charley Steiner, George Stephanopoulos, John Thorn, Joe Torre, Lance Van Auken, Rick Vaughn, Sarah Walton, Kevin J. Wells, George F. Will, Ruth W. Williams, and Don Zimmer.

Sources

Baseball Digest, 70th Anniversary Edition, September-October, 2012.

Baseball Reference.com (extensive use).

Bjarkman, Peter C. *The National Pastime:* "Lifting the Iron Curtain of Cuban Baseball."

Bloom, Barry. MLB.com: Dec. 9, 2013: "La Russa, Torre, Cox going to Hall of Fame."

Bradley, Mark. *Atlanta Journal-Constitution*, Feb. 2, 1996: "Turner Learned Owners Game."

Brokaw, Tom. *The Greatest Generation.* New York: Random House, 1998.

Bryant, Howard. *Juicing the Game.* New York: Viking Press, 2005.

Bush, George W. *Decision Points.* New York: Crown Publishers, 2010.

Cannon, Carl M., *The Atlantic Monthly*, May 2001: "The Oval Office and the Diamond."

Costello, Rory, Sam Hairston bio for SABR.

Dickson, Paul. *The Dickson Baseball Dictionary, Third Edition.* New York: W.W. Norton & Co., Inc., 2009.

Eradi, John. *Cincinnati Enquirer*, June 18, 2009: "Hairston closes the circle."

Gammons, Peter. *Sports Illustrated Vault*, Nov. 8, 1989. "A Hero Lives Here."

Gammons, Peter. *The Boston Globe*, Feb. 8, 1991: "Like father, like son, like grandson."

Geracie, Bud. *San Jose Mercury News*: "Tony La Russa was more 'grinder' than 'genius.'"

Hart, Simon. *Telegraph Media Group Limited*, Nov. 11, 2013: "Lance Armstrong pleads to be treated the same as all other cycling drugs cheats."

Heller, Dick. *The Washington Times*, May 9, 2005: "Ted Turner managed to shake up baseball in '77."

Hellmich, Nancy. *USA TODAY*, Feb. 20, 2003: "FDA awaits ephedra report after baseball player's death."

Helyar, John. *Lords of the Realm.* Norwalk, Connecticut: The Easton Press, 1994.

Hogan, Kenneth. *America's Ballparks.* Battle Ground, WA: Pediment Publishing, 2003.

Holtzman, Jerome. *The Commissioners.* New York: Total Sports, 1998.

Hrkach, Wendy. *The Morning Call*, Feb. 20, 1995.

Jehl, Douglas. *The New York Times*, Jan. 27, 1995.

Kaplan, Jim and Maisel, Ivan. *Sports Illustrated*, May 20, 1985: "The Commissioner Gets Tough."

Kates, Maxwell. Frank Robinson bio for SABR.

Kuhn, Bowie. *Hardball.* New York: Times Books, 1987.

Kuper, Simon. *Financial Times*, Nov. 13, 2011: "Michael Lewis and Billy Beane talk *Moneyball*."

Leiker, Ken. *Major League Baseball Memorable Moments.* New York: Ballantine Books, 2002.

Leventhal, Josh. *Take Me Out To The Ballpark.* New York: Black Dog & Leventhal Publishers, Inc., 2011.

Lewis, Michael. *Moneyball.* New York: W.W. Norton & Co., Ltd., 2003.

Lowe, John. *Detroit Free Press*, July 28, 1997: "Bell, Three favorite players, one big regret."

Madden, Bill. *Pride of October.* New York: Warner Books, 2003.

Madden, Bill. *Steinbrenner, The Last Lion of Baseball*. New York: HarperCollins Publishers, 2010.

Markusen, Bruce. Joe Coleman bio for SABR.

Miller, Scott. *Pioneer Planet.com*, March 23, 1999: "No political movement for Oliva."

Muder, Craig. *Memories and Dreams*, Baseball Hall of Fame, Spring 2009: "Henderson at Home in Any Era."

Murphy, Austin. *Sports Illustrated*, March 23, 1992: "Like Father, Like Son, Like…"

National Baseball Hall of Fame and Museum. *The National Baseball Hall of Fame Almanac, 2012 Edition.* Durham, NC: Baseball America, 2012.

Neuharth, Al. *Confessions of an S.O.B.* New York: Doubleday, 1989.

Odell, John. *Baseball As America.* Cooperstown, NY: National Baseball Hall of Fame and Museum, 2002.

Oldenburg, Ann. *USA TODAY*, Jan. 18, 2001: "The Bushes: Cut out from down-home fun."

Oliva, Tony and Fowler, Bob. *Tony O. The Trials and Triumphs of Tony Oliva.* New York: Hawthrone Books, 1973.

Olney, Buster. ESPN.com, Oct. 23, 2013: "Days of Superstar Managers are Over."

Passan, Jeff. *Yahoo Sports*, Nov. 18, 2011.

Presidents and America's Pastime: Selection of Baseball Documents from Presidential Libraries.

Raposo, Joe. *"There Used to be a Ballpark"* June 22, 1973 (Sung by Frank Sinatra, "Ol' Blue Eyes is Back" Album, arranged by Gordon Jenkins).

Robinson, Jackie and Duckett, Alfred. *I Never Had It Made.* New York: G.P. Putnam's Sons, 1972.

Robinson, Jackie. *A Life Remembered.* Norwalk, CT: The Easton Press, 1987.

Rogers III, C. Paul, Eddie Robinson bio for SABR.

Shaughnessy, Dan. *The Boston Globe*, May 21, 2004: "Baseball has been quite a boon to this family."

Shea, John. *San Francisco Chronicle*, Dec. 9, 2013: "Tony La Russa presided over dynamic era in Oakland."

Siwoff, Seymour. *The Elias Book of Baseball Records.* New York: Elias Sports Bureau, 2013.

Smith, Curt. *Storied Stadiums.* New York: Carroll & Graf Publishers, 2001.

Smith, Ron. *Heroes of the Hall.* St. Louis, MO: The Sporting News, 2002.

Sporting News, Archives of. *Baseball – 100 Years of the Modern Era: 1901–2000.* St. Louis, MO: Sporting News, 2001.

Staudohar, Paul D. *Monthly Labor Review*, March 1997.

Torre, Joe and Verducci, Tom. *The Yankee Years.* New York: Doubleday, 2009.

Treder, Steve. *The Hardball Times*, Nov. 21, 2006: "Out of Oakland."

Wancho, Joseph. Joey Jay bio for SABR.

Wancho, Joseph. Ray Boone bio for SABR.

Wells, Kevin J. *Washington Times Communities*, Oct. 10, 2013: "Willie Mays Aikens on career, drug use, prison, and returning."

Wikipedia.

Will, George F. *Men At Work.* New York: Macmillan Publishing Company, 1990.

Zimmer, Don and Madden, Bill. *The Zen of Zim: Baseballs, Beanballs, and Bosses.* New York: Thomas Dunne Books, 2004.

Zimmer, Don and Madden, Bill. *Zim: A Baseball Life.* New York: Total Sports Illustrated, 2001.

About the Author

Hal Bodley, dean of American baseball writers, is senior correspondent for MLB.com and has covered the game since 1958. He is the former baseball editor and columnist for *USA TODAY* and is a founder and former president of the Associated Press Sports Editors Association. He has served as a broadcast analyst for CBS, CNN, and NBC. He has won 30 regional and national writing awards and was elected to the Delaware Sports Hall of Fame and the Delaware Baseball Hall of Fame. He is the co-author of *Countdown to Cobb: My Diary of the Record Breaking 1985 Season,* with Pete Rose, and author of *The Team That Wouldn't Die,* on the world champion 1980 Phillies.